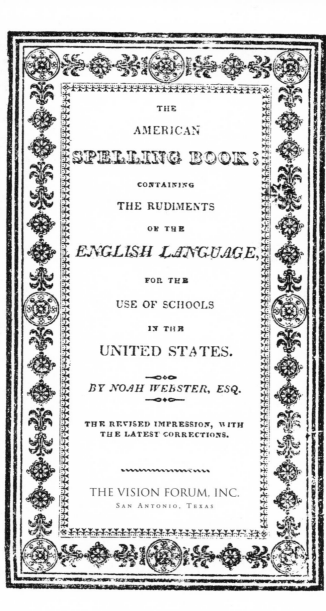

THE

AMERICAN

SPELLING BOOK;

CONTAINING

THE RUDIMENTS

OF THE

ENGLISH LANGUAGE,

FOR THE

USE OF SCHOOLS

IN THE

UNITED STATES.

BY NOAH WEBSTER, ESQ.

THE REVISED IMPRESSION, WITH
THE LATEST CORRECTIONS.

THE VISION FORUM, INC.
San Antonio, Texas

SECOND PRINTING

COPYRIGHT © 2002, 2003 THE VISION FORUM, INC.
All Rights Reserved

"Where there is no vision, the people perish."

THE VISION FORUM, INC.
4719 Blanco Rd., San Antonio, Texas 78212
1-800-440-0022
www.visionforum.com

UNABRIDGED REPRINT OF
NINETEENTH CENTURY EDITION

PRINTED IN THE UNITED STATES OF AMERICA

ISBN 1-929241-16-X

9 781929 241163

PUBLISHER'S NOTE

The great American educator Noah Webster first published *A Grammatical Institute of the English Language*, otherwise known as the *Blue Back Speller*, in 1783. His goal was to provide a uniquely American, Christ-centered approach to training children. Little did he know that this remarkable gem would become the staple for parents and educators for more than a century and would help to build the most literate nation in the history of the West. Many of the Founding Fathers used this book to home school their children, including Benjamin Franklin who taught his granddaughter to read, spell, and pronounce words using "Old Blue Back."

Vision Forum is pleased to make this wonderful Christian classics available as part of our Patriotic Textbook Series.

To God Be the Glory,
Douglas W. Phillips, Esq.
President, The Vision Forum, Inc.

PREFACE.

THE *American Spelling Book*, or first Part of a Grammatical Institute of the English language, when first published, encountered an opposition, which few new publications have sustained with success. It however maintained its ground, and its reputation has been gradually extended and established, until it has become the principal elementary book in the United States. In a great part of the northern States, it is the only book of the kind used; it is much used in the middle and southern States; and its annual sales indicate a large and increasing demand. Its merit is evinced not only by this general use, but by a remarkable fact, that, in many attempts made to rival it, the compilers have all constructed their works on a similar plan; some of them have most unwarrantably and illegally copied a considerable part of the tables, with little or no alteration; and others have altered them, by additions, mutilations, and subdivisions, numerous and perplexing. In most instances, this species of injustice has been discountenanced by the citizens of the United States, and the public sentiment has protected the original work, more effectually than the penalties of the law.*

Gratitude to the public, as well as a desire to furnish schools with a more complete and well digested system of elements has induced me to embrace the opportunity when the first patent expires, to revise the work, and give it all the improvement which the experience of many teachers, and my own observations and reflections have suggested. In the execution of this design, care has been taken to preserve the scheme of pronunciation, and the substance of the former work. Most of the tables, having stood the test of experience, are considered as susceptible of little improvement or amendment. A few alterations are made, with a view to accommodate the

---

* The sales of the *American Spelling Book*, since its first publication, amount to more than *Five Millions* of copies, and they are annually increasing. One great advantage experienced in using this work, is the simplicity of the scheme of pronunciation, which exhibits the sounds of the letters with sufficient accuracy, without a mark over each vowel. The multitude of characters in Perry's scheme renders it far too complex and perplexing to be useful to children, confusing the eye, without enlightening the understanding. Nor is there the least necessity for a figure over each vowel, as in Walker, Sheridan, and other authors. In nine-tenths of the words in our language, a correct pronunciation is better taught by a natural division of the syllables, and a direction for placing the accent, than by a minute and endless repetition of characters. *March*, 1818.

work to the most accurate rules of pronunciation, and most general usage of speaking; as also to correct some errors which had crept into the work. A perfect standard of pronunciation, in a living language, is not to be expected: and when the best English Dictionaries differ from each other, in several hundred, probably a thousand words, where are we to seek for undisputed rules? and how can we arrive at perfect uniformity?

The rules respecting accent, prefixed to the former work, are found to be too lengthy and complex, to answer any valuable purpose in a work intended for children; they are therefore omitted. The geographical tables are thrown into a different form; and the abridgment of grammar is omitted. Geography and grammar are sciences that require distinct treatises, and schools are furnished with them in abundance. It is believed to be more useful to confine this work to its proper objects,—the teaching of the first elements of the language, spelling and reading. On this subject the opinion of many judicious persons concurs with my own.

The improvements made in this work chiefly consist in a great number of new tables. Some of them are intended to exhibit the manner in which derivative words, and the variations of nouns, adjectives and verbs, are formed. The examples of this sort cannot fail to be very useful; as children who may be well acquainted with a word in the singular number, or positive degree, may be perplexed when they see it in the plural number, or comparative form. The examples of derivation, will accustom youth to observe the manner, in which various branches spring from one radical word, and thus lead their minds to some knowledge of the formation of the language, and the manner in which syllables are added or prefixed to vary the sense of words.

In the familiar lessons for reading, care has been taken to express ideas in plain, but not in vulgar language; and to combine, with the familiarity of objects, useful truth and practical principles.

In a copious list of names of places, rivers, lakes, mountains, &c. which are introduced into this work, no labor has been spared to exhibit their just orthography and pronunciation, according to the analogies of our language, and the common usages of the country. The orthography of Indian names has not, in every instance, been well adjusted by American authors. Many of these names still retain the French orthography, found in the writings of the first discoverers or early travellers; but the practice of writing such words in the French manner ought to be discountenanced. How does an unlettered American know the pronunciation of the names, *Ouisconsin* or *Ouabasche*, in this French dress? Would he suspect the pronunciation to be Wisconsin and

Waubosh? Our citizens ought not to be thus perplexed with an orthography to which they are strangers. Nor ought the harsh guttural sounds of the natives to be retained in such words as Shawangunk, and many others. Where popular practice has softened and abridged words of this kind, the change has been made in conformity to the genius of our language, which is accommodated to a civilized people; and the orthography ought to be conformed to the practice of speaking. The true pronunciation of the name of a place, is that which prevails in and near the place. I have always sought for this, but am apprehensive, that in some instances, my information may not be correct. It has however been my endeavor to give the true pronunciation, in the appropriate English characters.

The importance of correctness and uniformity, in the several impressions of a book of such general use, has suggested the propriety of adopting effectual measures to insure these desirable objects; and it is believed that such measures are taken, as will render all the future impressions of this work, uniform in the pages, well executed and perfectly correct.

In the progress of society and improvement, some gradual changes must be expected in a living language; and corresponding alterations in elementary books of instruction, become indispensable; but it is desirable that these alterations should be as few as possible, for they occasion uncertainty and inconvenience. And although perfect uniformity in speaking, is not probably attainable in any living language, yet it is to be wished, that the youth of our country may be as little as possible, perplexed with various differing systems and standards. Whatever may be the difference of opinion, among individuals, respecting a few particular words, or the particular arrangement of a few classes of words, the general interest of education requires, that a disposition to multiply books and systems for teaching the language of the country, should not be indulged to an unlimited extent. On this disposition, however, the public sentiment alone can impose restraint.

As the first part of the Institute met with the general approbation of my fellow citizens, it is presumed the labor bestowed upon this work, in correcting and improving the system, will render it still more acceptable to the public, by facilitating the education of youth, and enabling teachers to instil into their minds, with the first rudiments of the language, some just ideas of religion, morals, and domestic economy.

N. W.

New-Haven, 1803.

ANALYSIS OF SOUNDS

IN THE

ENGLISH LANGUAGE.

—◆◆◆—

LANGUAGE, in its more limited sense, is the expression of ideas by articulate sounds   In a more general sense, the word denotes all sounds by which animals express their feelings, in such a manner as to be understood by their own species.

Articulate sounds are those which are formed by the human voice, in pronouncing letters, syllables and words, and constitute the *spoken* language, which is addressed to the *ear*. Letters are the marks of sounds, and the first elements of *written* language, which is presented to the *eye*.

In a perfect language, every simple sound would be expressed by a distinct character; and no character would have more than one sound.   But languages are not thus perfect; and the English Language, in particular, is, in these respects, extremely irregular.

The letters used in writing, when arranged in a certain customary order, compose what is called an *Alphabet*.

The English Alphabet consists of twenty-six letters, or single characters; and for want of others, certain simple sounds are represented by two letters united.

The letters or single characters are, a, b, c, d, e, f, g, h, i, j, k, l, m, n, o, p, q, r, s, t, u, v, w, x, y, z.   The compound characters representing distinct sounds are, ch, sh, th.   There is also a distinct sound expressed by *ng*, as in *long;* and another by *s* or *z*, as in *fusion, azure*, which sound might be represented by *zh*.

Letters are of two kinds, *vowels* and *consonants*.

A vowel is a simple articulate sound. formed without the help of another letter, by opening the mouth in a particular manner and begun and completed with the same position of the organs; as. *a, e, o*.   The letters which represent these sounds are six; *a, e. i, o, u, y*.   But each of these characters is used to express two or more sounds.

The following are the vowel sounds in the English Language—of *a*, as in late, ask, ball, hat, what.

> of *e*, in mete, met.
> of *i*, in find, pit,
> of *o*, in note, not, move.
> of *u*, in truth, but, bush.
> of *y*, in chyle, pity.

The vowels have a long and a short sound, or quantity; and the different quantities are represented by different letters. Thus,

Long.
a, in late,	{ when shortened, is expressed }	by *e*, as in let.
ee, in feet,		by *i*, in fit, & *y* in pity.
oo, in pool,		by *u*, in pull, & *oo* in wool.
a, in hall,		by *o*, in holly, and *a* in wallow.

That the sounds of *a* in *late* and *e* in *let* are only a modification of the same vowel, may be easily understood by attending to the manner of forming the sounds; for in both words, the aperture of the mouth and the configuration of the organs are the same. This circumstance proves the sameness of the sound or vowel, in the two words, though differing in time or quantity.

A consonant is a letter which has no sound, or an imperfect one, without the help of a vowel. The consonants which are entirely silent, interrupt the voice by closing the organs; as b, d, g hard, k, p, t, which are called *mutes;* as in eb, ed, eg, ek, ep, et.

The consonants which do not entirely interrupt all sound by closing the organs, are f, l, m, n, r, s, v, z, which are all half vowels or semi-vowels.—To these may be added the sounds of sh, th, zh, and ng. in esh, eth, ezh, ing, which our language has no single characters to express.

A dipthong is the union of two simple sounds uttered in one breath or articulation. The two sounds do not strictly form one; for there are two different positions of the organs, and two distinct sounds; but the transition from one to the other is so rapid, that the distinction is scarcely perceived, and the sound is therefore considered as compound. Dipthongal sounds are sometimes represented by two letters, as in *voice. joy,* and sometimes by one, as in *defy;* the sound of *y,* in the latter word, if prolonged, terminates in *e,* and is really dipthongal.

A tripthong is a union of three vowels in a syllable; but it may be questioned whether in any English word, we pronounce three vowels in a single articulation. In the word *adieu*, the three vowels are not distinctly sounded.

B has but one sound, as in bite.

C is always sounded like *k* or *s*—like *k* before *a*, *o*, and *u*—and like *s* before *e*, *i*, and *y*. Thus,

ca, ce, ci, co, cu, cy.
ka, se, si, ko, ku, sy

At the end of words it is always hard like *k*, as in *public*. When followed by *i* or *e* before a vowel, the syllable slides into the sound of *sh*; as in cetaceous, gracious, social, which are pronounced cetashus, grashus, soshal

D has only one sound, as in dress, bold.

F has its own proper sound, as in life, fever, except in *of*, where it has the sound of *v*.

G before *a*, *o*, and *u*, has always its hard sound, as in gave, go, gun.

Before *e*, *i*, and *y*, it has the same hard sound in some words, and in others, the sound of *j*. But these varieties are incapable of being reduced to any general rule, and are to be learnt only by practice, observation, and a dictionary, in which the sounds are designated.

H can hardly be said to have any sound, but it denotes an aspiration or impulse of breath, which modifies the sound of the following vowel. as in heart, heave.

I is a vowel, as in fit; or a consonant as in bullion.

J is the mark of a compound sound, or union of sounds, which may be represented by *dzh*, or the soft *g*, as in jelly.

K has but one sound, as in king; and before *n* is always silent, as in know

L has but one sound, as in lame. It is silent before *k*, as in walk.

M has but one sound, as in man, and is never silent.

N has but one sound, as in not, and is silent after *m*, as in hymn.

P has one uniform sound, as in pit.

Q has the power of *k*, and is always followed by *u*, as in question.

R has one sound only, as in barrel.

S has the sound of *c*, as in so; of *z*, as in rose—and when followed by *i* preceding a vowel, the syllable has the sound of *sh*, as in mission; or *zh*, as in osier.

T has its proper sound, as in *turn*, at the beginning of words and end of syllables. In all the terminations in *tion*, and *tial*, *ti* have the sound of *sh*, as in nation, nuptial); ex cept when preceded by *s* or *x*, in which cases they have the sound of *ch*, as in question, mixtion.

U has the properties of a consonant and vowel, in union, unanimity, &c.

V has uniformly one sound, as in voice, live, and is never silent.

W has the power of a vowel, as in dwell; or a consonant, as in well, will.

X has the sound of *ks*, as in wax; or of *gz*, as in exist, and in other words, when followed by an accented syllable beginning with a vowel. In the beginning of Greek names, it has the sound of *z*, as in Xerxes, Xenophon.

Y is a vowel, as in vanity; a dipthong, as in defy; or a consonant, as in young.

Z has its own sound usually, as in zeal, freeze.

Ch have the sound of *tsh* in words of English origin, as in chip—in some words of French original, they have the sound of *sh*, as in machine—and some words of Greek origin, the sound of *k*, as in chorus.

Gh have the sound of *f*, as in laugh, or are silent, as in light.

Ph have the sound of *f*, as in philosophy; except in Stephen, where the sound is that of *v*.

Ng have a nasal sound, as in sing; but when *e* follows *g*, the latter takes the sound of *j*, as in range. In the words, longer, stronger, younger, the sound of the *g* is doubled, and the last syllable is sounded as if written long-ger, &c.

Sh has one sound only, as in shell; but its use is often supplied by *ti*, *si*, and *ce*, before a vowel, as in motion, gracious, cetaceous.

Th has two sounds, aspirate and vocal—aspirate, as in think, bath—vocal, as in those, that, bathe.

Sc before *a, o, u,* and *r*, are pronounced like *sk*, as in scale, scoff, sculpture, scribble: before *e, i, y* like soft *c*, or *s*, as in scene, sceptic, science, Scythian. Thus pronounced,

sca, sce, sci, sco, scu, scy.

ska, se, si, sko, sku, sy

Formation of Words and Sentences.

Letters form syllables: syllables form words, and words form sentences, which compose a discourse.

A syllable is a letter or a union of letters, which can be uttered at one impulse of voice.

A word of one syllable is called a monosyllable.

of two syllables	a dissyllable.
of three syllables	a trisyllable.
of many syllables	a polysyllable.

Of Accent, Emphasis, and Cadence.

Accent is a forcible stress or impulse of voice on a letter or syllable, distinguishing it from others in the same word. When it falls on a vowel, it prolongs the sound, as in glory; when it falls on a consonant, the preceding vowel is short, as in habit.

The general rule by which accent is regulated, is, that the stress of voice falls on that syllable of a word. which renders the articulation most easy to the speaker, and most agreeable to the hearer—By this rule has the accent of most words been imperceptibly established by long and universal consent.

When a word consists of three or more syllables, the ease of speaking requires usually a secondary accent, of less forcible utterance than the primary, but clearly distinguishable from the pronunciation of unaccented syllables; as superfluity, literary.

In many compound words, the parts of which are important words of themselves, there is very little distinction of accent, as ink-stand, church-yard.

Emphasis is a particular force of utterance given to a particular word in a sentence, on account of its importance.

Cadence is a fall or modulation of the voice in reading or speaking, especially at the end of a sentence.

Words are simple or compound, primitive or derivative.

A simple word cannot be divided, without destroying the sense; as man, child, house, charity, faith.

A compound word is formed by two or more words; as chimney-piece, book-binder.

Primitive words are such as are not derived, but constitute a radical stock from which others are formed; as grace, hope, charm.

Derivative words are those which are formed of a primitive, and some termination or additional syllable; as grace-less, hope-ful, charm-ing, un-welcome.

Spelling is the art or practice of writing or reading the proper letters of a word; called also orthography. In forming tables for learners, the best rule to be observed, is, to divide the syllables in such a manner as to guide the learner by the sound of the letters, to the sound of the words; that is, to divide them as they are divided in a just pronunciation

Key to the following Work.

	Long.			Short aw.	
1	**1**	**1**	**5**	**5**	**5**
a	name,	late.	a	what,	was.
e *or* ee	here,	feet.	o	not,	from.
i	time,	find.		Oo proper.	
o	note,	fort.	**6**	**6**	**6**
u *or* ew	tune,	new.	o *or* oo	move,	room.
y	dry,	defy.		Oo Short.	
			7	**7**	**7**
	Short.		oo	book,	stood.
2	**2**	**2**	u	bush,	full.
a	man,	hat.		Short u.	
e	men,	let.	**8**	**8**	**8**
i	pit,	pin.	i	sir.	bird.
u	tun,	but.	o	come,	love.
y	glory,	Egypt.	e	her.	
				Long a.	
	Broad a or aw.		**9**	**9**	**9**
3	**3**	**3**	e	there,	vein.
a	bald,	tall.		Long e.	
o	cost,	sought.	**10**	**10**	**10**
aw	law.		i	fatigue,	pique.
			oi	} dipthong; voice, joy.	
	Flat a.		oy		
4	**4**	**4**	ou	} dipthong; loud, now.	
a	ask,	part.	ow		

EXPLANATION OF THE KEY.

A figure stands as the invariable representative of a certain sound. The figure 1 represents the long sound of the letters, *a, e, i, o, u,* or *ew,* and *y ;* number 2, the short sound of the same characters ; number 3, marks the sound of broad *a,* as in *hall ;* number 4, represents the sound of *a,* in *father ;* number 5, represents the short sound of broad *a,* as in *not, what ;* number 6, represents the sound of *o* in *more,* commonly expressed by *oo;* number 7, represents the short sound of *oo* in *root, bush ;* number 8, represents the sound of *u* short, made by *e, i,* and *o,* as in *her, bird, come*, pronounced *hur*, *burd*, *cum*; number 9, represents the first sound of *a*, made by *e*, as in *their*, *vein*. pronounced *thare*, *vane*; number 10, represents the French sound of *i*, which is the same as *e* long.

The sounds of the dipthongs of *oi* and *ou* are not represented by figures; these have one invariable sound, and are placed before the words where they occur in the tables.

Silent letters are printed in Italic characters. Thus, in *head*, *goal*, *build*, *people*, *fight*, the Italic letters have no sound.

S, when printed in Italic, is not silent, but pronounced like *z*, as in *devise*, pronounced *devize*.

The letter *e* at the end of words of more syllables than one, is almost always silent: but serves often to lengthen a foregoing vowel, as in *bid*, *bide*; to soften *c*, as in *notice*; or to soften *g*, as in *homage*; or to change the sound of *th* from the first to the second, as in *bath*, *bathe*. In the following work, when *e* final lengthens the foregoing vowel, that is, give it its first sound, it is printed in a Roman character, as in *fate*; but in all other cases it is printed in Italic, except in table 39.

Ch have the English sound, as in *charm*; except in the 38th and 39th tables.

The sounds of *th* in *this* and *thou*, are all distinguished in the 12th and 37th tables; except in numeral adjectives.

The sound of *aw* is invariably that of broad *a*, and that of *ew* nearly the same as *u* long.

N. B. Although one character is sufficient to express a simple sound, yet the combinations *ee*, *aw*, *ew*, *oo*, are so well known to express certain sounds, that it was judged best to print both letters in Roman characters. *Ck* and *ss* are also printed in Roman characters, though one alone would be sufficient to express the sound.

" Delightful task, to rear the tender thought,
And teach the young idea how to shoot."

A B C D E F G H I J
K L M N O P Q R S
T U V W X Y Z

a b c d e f g h i j k l m n
o p q r s t u v w x y z &
æ œ fi ff fl ffl ffi

A B C D E F G H I
J K L M N O P Q R
S T U V W X Y Z
1 2 3 4 5 6 7 8 9 0

The ALPHABET.

Roman Letters.		Italic.		Names of Letters.
a	A	*a*	*A*	a
b	B	*b*	*B*	be
c	C	*c*	*C*	ce
d	D	*d*	*D*	de
e	E	*e*	*E*	e
f	F	*f*	*F*	ef
g	G	*g*	*G*	je
h	H	*h*	*H*	he, *or* aytch
i	I	*i*	*I*	i
j	J	*j*	*J*	ja
k	K	*k*	*K*	ka
l	L	*l*	*L*	el
m	M	*m*	*M*	em
n	N	*n*	*N*	en
o	O	*o*	*O*	o
p	P	*p*	*P*	pe
q	Q	*q*	*Q*	cu
r	R	*r*	*R*	ar
s	S	*s*	*S*	es
t	T	*t*	*T*	te
u	U	*u*	*U*	u
v	V	*v*	*V*	ve
w	W	*w*	*W*	oo
x	X	*x*	*X*	eks
y	Y	*y*	*Y*	wi *or* ye
z	Z	*z*	*Z*	ze
&*		&*		and

Double LETTERS.

ff, ffl, fi, fl, ffi.

* This is not a letter, but a character standing for *and.* Chil
dren therefore should be taught to call it *and;* not *and-per-se.*

TABLE I.

Lesson I.

ba	be	bi	bo	bu	by
ca	ce*	ci*	co	cu	cy*
da	de	di	do	du	dy
fa	fe	fi	fo	fu	fy
ka	ke	ki	ko	ku	ky

Lesson II.

ga	ge	gi	go	gu	gy
ha	he	hi	ho	hu	hy
ma	me	mi	mo	mu	my
na	ne	ni	no	nu	ny
ra	re	ri	ro	ru	ry
ta	te	ti	to	tu	ty
wa	we	wi	wo	wu	wy

Lesson III.

la	le	li	lo	lu	ly
pa	pe	pi	po	pu	py
sa	se	si	so	su	sy
za	ze	zi	zo	zu	zy

Lesson IV.

ab	eb	ib	ob	ub
ac	ec	ic	oc	uc
ad	ed	id	od	ud
af	ef	if	of	uf
al	el	il	ol	ul

Lesson V.

ag	eg	ig	og	ug
am	em	im	om	um
an	en	in	on	un
ap	ep	ip	op	up
as	es	is	os	us
av	ev	iv	ov	uv
ax	ex	ix	ox	ux

Lesson VI.

ak	ek	ik	ok	uk
at	et	it	ot	ut
ar	er	ir	or	ur
az	ez	iz	oz	uz

Lesson VII.

bla	ble	bli	blo	blu
cla	cle	cli	clo	clu
pla	ple	pli	plo	plu
fla	fle	fli	flo	flu
va	ve	vi	vo	vu

Lesson VIII.

bra	bre	bri	bro	bru
cra	cre	cri	cro	cru
pra	pre	pri	pro	pru
gra	gre	gri	gro	gru
pha	phe	phi	pho	phu

Lesson IX.

cha	che	chi	cho	chu	chy
dra	dre	dri	dro	dru	dry
fra	fre	fri	fro	fru	fry
gla	gle	gli	glo	glu	gly

Lesson X.

sla	sle	sli	slo	slu	sly
qua	que	qui	quo		
sha	she	shi	sho	shu	shy
spa	spe	spi	spo	spu	spy

Lesson XI.

sta	ste	sti	sto	stu	sty
sca	sce	sci	sco	scu	scy
tha	the	thi	tho	thu	thy
tra	tre	tri	tro	tru	try

* They should be taught to pronounce, *ce, ci, cy,* like *se, si, sy.*

LESSON XII.

spla	sple	spli	splo	splu	sply
spra	spre	spri	spro	spru	spry
stra	stre	stri	stro	stru	stry
swa	swe	swi	swo	swu	swy

TABLE II.

Words of one syllable.

Note. A figure placed over the first word, marks the sound of the vowel in all that follow in that column, until contradicted by another figure.

LESSON I.

Băg	bĭg	bŏg	bŭg	dĕn	căp	bĭt	dŏt
fag	dig	dog	dug	hen	gap	cit	got
cag	fig	fog	hug	men	lap	hit	hot
gag	gig	hog	lug	pen	map	pit	jot
hag	pig	jog	mug	ten	rap	sit	lot
rag	wig	log	tug	wen	tap	wit	not

LESSON II.

Măn	fŏb	tăd	bĕd	bĭd	fŏp	bĕt	bŭt
can	job	had	fed	did	hop	get	cut
pan	mob	lad	led	lid	lop	let	hut
ran	rob	mad	red	hid	mop	met	nut
van	sob	sad	wed	rid	top	yet	put

LESSON III.

Bĕlt	gĭlt	bănd	blĕd	brăg	clŏd	brăd
melt	hilt	hand	bred	drag	plod	clad
felt	milt	land	fled	flag	snod	glad
pelt	jilt	sand	shed	stag	trod	shad

LESSON IV.

Clŏg	glŭt	blăb	chŭb	dămp	bŭmp	bĕnd
flog	shut	drab	club	camp	jump	lend
frog	smut	crab	drub	lamp	lump	mend
grog	slut	scab	grub	vamp	pump	send

B 2

Lesson V.

Bìnd	bóld	càll	bìll	bènt	bèst	brìm
find	hold	fall	fill	dent	lest	grim
mind	fold	gall	hill	lent	nest	skim
kind	sold	hall	kill	sent	jest	swim
wind	gold	tall	mill	went	pest	trim

Lesson VI.

Làce	dìce	fàde	bìde	càge	bàke	dìne
mace	nice	lade	ride	page	cake	fine
trace	nice	made	side	rage	make	pine
pace	rice	wade	wide	wage	wake	wine

Lesson VII.

Gàle	càpe	pìpe	cópe	dìre	dàte	drìve
pale	rape	ripe	hope	hire	hate	five
sale	tape	wipe	rope	fire	fate	hive
vale	ape	type	pope	wire	grate	rive

Lesson VIII.

Dote	file	dame	fare	bore	bone	nose
mote	bile	fame	mare	sore	cone	dose
note	pile	came	rare	tore	hone	hose
vote	vile	name	tare	wore	tone	rose

TABLE III.

Lesson I.

Blànk	blùsh	flèct	bràce	price	brine
flank	flush	sheet	chace	slice	shine
frank	plush	street	grace	spice	swine
prank	crush	greet	space	twice	twine

Lesson II.

Bànd	blèss	crìme	bróke	blàde	blàme
grand	dress	chime	choke	spade	flame
stand	press	prime	cloke	trade	shame
strand	stress	slime	smoke	shade	frame

LESSON III.

Bràke	glàre	bràve	hènce	mìnce	blèed
drake	share	crave	fence	since	breed
flake	snare	grave	pence	prince	speed
spake	spare	slave	sense	rinse	steed

LESSON IV.

And	ìll	àge	hìs	rìch	lèss	dùke	lìfe
act	ink	aim	has	held	mess	mule	wife
apt	fact	aid	hast	gift	kiss	rule	safe
ell	fan	ice	hath	dull	miss	time	male
ebb	left	ale	add	till	tush	tune	save
egg	self	ace	elf	will	hush	mute	here
end	else	ape	ren	well	desk	maze	robe

LESSON V.

Glàde	snàke	tract	clànk	clàmp	blàck
grade	glaze	pact	crank	champ	crack
shave	craze	plant	shank	cramp	match
wave	prate	sang	plank	spasm	patch
quake	slate	fang	clump	splash	fetch
stage	shape	rang	thump	crash	vetch

LESSON VI.

Mìne	sìre	strìfe	brìde	brìck	strìve
spine	quire	fife	chide	kick	spike
vine	spire	trite	glide	chick	splice
gripe	mire	quite	pride	click	strike
snipe	smite	squire	vice	lick	ride
stripe	spite	spike	trice	stick	wide

LESSON VII.

Examples of the formation of the plural from the singular, and of other derivatives.

name,	names	camp,	camps	slave,	slaves
dame,	dames	clamp,	clamps	brave,	braves
gale,	gales	lamp,	lamps	stave,	staves

scale,	scales	scalp,	scalps	mate,	mates
cape,	capes	map,	maps	state,	states
grape,	grapes	plant,	plants	mind,	minds
crane,	cranes	plank,	planks	bind,	binds
shade,	shades	flag,	flags	snare,	snares
grade,	grades	bank,	banks	snake,	snakes

LESSON VIII.

cake,	cakes	chap,	chaps	shake,	shakes
flake,	flakes	flank,	flanks	spade,	spades
hope,	hopes	shine,	shines	pipe,	pipes
note,	notes	slope,	slopes	wire,	wires
blot,	blots	fold,	folds	hive,	hives
cube,	cubes	club,	clubs	pine,	pines
grave,	graves	vote,	votes	fade,	fades
street,	streets	cone,	cones	mill,	mills
sheet,	sheets	bone,	bones	hill,	hills

LESSON IX.

side,	sides	blank,	blanks	mare,	mares
vale,	vales	choke,	chokes	tare,	tares
wife,	wives	cloke,	clokes	grate,	grates
life,	lives	smoke,	smokes	smite,	smites
hive,	hives	flame,	flames	brick,	bricks
drive,	drives	frame,	frames	kick,	kicks
go,	goes	stand,	stands	stick,	sticks
wo,	woes	drove,	droves	bride,	brides
do,	does	robe,	robes	fire,	fires
add,	adds	spot,	spots	smell,	smells
lad,	lads	flag,	flags	swim,	swims

TABLE IV.

Easy words of two syllables, accented on the first.

When the stress of voice falls on a vowel, it is necessarily long, and is marked by the figure 1. When the stress of voice falls on a consonant, the preceding vowel is necessarily short, and is marked by figure 2.

No figures are placed over the vowels in unaccented syllables, because they are short. It must be observed, however, that in unaccented terminating syllables, almost all vowels are pronounced like *i* and *u* short. Thus,

al *is pronounced* ul,   *rural rurul,*
et   it,   *fillet fillit.*

This is the general rule in the language; originating doubtless from this cause, that short *i* and *u* are pronounced with a less aperture or opening of the mouth, with less exertions of the organs, and consequently with more ease than the other vowels in these terminating syllables; for in order to pronounce them right, nothing more is requisite than to lay a proper stress of the voice on the accented syllable, and pronounce the unaccented syllables with more ease and rapidity. When any of these terminations are accented, as some of them are, the vowel retains its own sound; as, *compel, lament, depress,* &c.

The figures are placed over the vowels of the accented syllables; and one figure marks all the words that follow, till it is contradicted by another figure.

Bà ker	glo ry	ne gro	sa cred
bri er	gi ant	o ver	se cret
ci der	gra vy	pa gan	sha dy
cra zy	gru' el	pa per	si lent
cri er	ho ly	pa pist	so ber
cru el	hu man	pi lot	spi der
di al	i cy	pli ant	sto ry
di et	i dol	po et	stu dent
du ty	i vy	pre cept	stu pid
dy er	ju ry	pru dent	ta per
dra per	ju lep	qui et	tra der
fa tal	la dy	ra ker	ti dings
fe ver	la zy	re al	to ry
fi nal	le gal	ri der	to tal
fla grant	li ar	ri ot	tri al
flu ent	li on	ru by	tru ant
fo cus	ma ker	ru in	tu mult
fru gal	mo dish	ru ler	tu tor
fu el	mo ment	ru ral	va cant

va grant	cut ler	ham let	mut ter
va ry	dan ger	han sel	num ber
vi per	dif fer	hap py	nut meg
vi tal	din ner	hin der	nurs ling
vo cal	drum mer	hun dred	pam per
wa fer	el der	hunt er	pan nel
wa ges	em bers	in sect	pan try
wa ger	em blem	in step	pat tern
wo ful	en ter	in to	pat ron
ab bot	fac tor	jest er	pen cil
act or	fag got	ken nel	pen ny
ad der	fan cy	kin dred	pep per
ad vent	fan tom	king dom	pil lar
al um	fat ling	kins man	pil fer
am ber	fer ret	lad der	pil grim
an gel	fil let	lan tern	plum met
bal lad	flan nel	lap pet	pup py
bank er	flat ter	lat ter	ram mer
ban ter	flut ter	let ter	ran som
bap tist	fran tic	lim ber	rec tor
bat ter	fun nel	lim ner	rem nant
bet ter	gal lop	lit ter	ren der
bit ter	gam mon	luck y	ren net
blun der	gan der	mam mon	rub bish
buf fet	gar ret	man na	sad ler
bur gess	gen try	man ner	sal lad
car rot	gib bet	mat ron	sand y
chan nel	gip sy	mem ber	sat in
chap man	glim mer	mer ry	scan dal
chap ter	glit ter	mill er	scat ter
chat ter	gul let	mit ten	sel dom
chil dren	gun ner	mur der	sel fish
chil ly	gus set	mud dy	sen tence
cin der	gut ter	mur mur	shat ter

shep herd	tan ner	wed ding	hor rid
shil ling	tat ler	wil ful	joc ky
sig nal	tem per	will ing	jol ly
sil ver	ten der	wis dom	mot to
sin ner	ten dril	árt less	on set
slat tern	ten ter	art ist	of fer
slen der	tim ber	af ter	of fice
slum ber	trench er	chŏp per	pot ter
smug gler	trum pet	com ment	rob ber
spin et	tum bler	com mon	sot tish
spir it	tur ky	con duct	clĕr gy
splen did	vel lum	con cord	er rand
splen dor	vel vet	con gress	her mit
splin ter	ves sel	con quest	ker nel
stam mer	vic tim	con sul	mer cy
sub ject	vul gar	con vert	per fect
sud den	ug ly	doc tor	per son
suf fer	ul cer	dross y	ser mon
sul len	un der	dol lar	ser pent
sul try	up per	fod der	serv ant
sum mon	ut most	fol ly	ver min
tal ly	ut ter	fop pish	ven om

---◦✳◦---

TABLE V.

Easy words of two syllables, accented on the second.

N. B. In general, when a vowel in an unaccented syllable, stands alone or ends a syllable,* it has its first sound, as in *protect:* yet as we do not dwell upon the vowel, it is short and weak. When the vowel, in such syllables, is joined to a consonant, it has its second sound; as *address.*

* But if a vowel unaccented ends the word, it has its second sound, as in city.

A báse	a like	a maze	at tire
a bide	al lude	as pire	be fore
a dore	a lone	a tone	be have

be hold	fore seen	trans late	di rect
com ply	im brue	un bind	dis band
com pute	im pale	un told	dis miss
com plete	in cite	un fold	dis sent
con fine	in flame	un glue	dis tinct
con jure	in trude	un kind	dis trust
con sume	in sure	un lace	dis tract
con trol	in vite	un ripe	dis turb
cre ate	mis name	un safe	ef fect
de cide	mis place	ab rupt	e mit
de clare	mis rule	ab surd	en camp
de duce	mis take	ac cept	en rich
de fy	mo rose	ad dict	e vent
de fine	par take	ad dress	e vince
de grade	per spire	ad mit	ful fil
de note	po lite	a mend	fi nance
de pute	pre pare	a midst	gal lant
de rive	pro mote	ar range	him self
dis like	re bate	as cend	im pend
dis place	re buke	be set	im plant
dis robe	re cite	ca nal	im press
dis taste	re cline	col lect	im print
di vine	re duce	com pel	in cur
e lope	re late	con duct	in dent
en dure	re ly	con tend	in fect
en force	re mind	con tent	in fest
en gage	re plete	cor rect	in flict
en rage	re vere	cor rupt	in stil
en rol	se duce	de duct	in struct
en sue	sub lime	de fect	in vest
en tice	su pine	de fend	mis give
en tire	su preme	de press	mis print
e vade	sur vive	de range	mis trust
for sworn	tra duce	de tect	mo lest

neg lect	re press	un bend	re volve
ob struct	re tract	un fit	re volt
oc cur	re trench	un hinge	de spond
of fence	ro bust	un hurt	un lock
o mit	ro mance	un man	con cert
op press	se dan	de bar	de fer
per mit	se lect	de part	di vert
por tend	sub ject	dis arm	in verse
pre tend	sub mit	dis card	in vert
pre dict	sub tract	em balm	per vert
pro ject	sus pense	em bark	per verse
pro tect	trans act	en chant	re fer
pro test	trans cend	en large	con fer
re cant	trans gress	huz za	de ter
re fit	trans plant	un arm	in fer
re lax	tre pan	un bar	in ter
re mit	un apt	ab hor	in tend

———◦✳◦———

TABLE VI.

Easy words of three syllables; the full accent on the first, and a weak accent on the third.

Cru ci fix	lu na cy	si mon y	ad a mant
cru el ty	no ta ry	stu pi fy	am i ty
de cen cy	nu mer al	tu te lar	am nes ty
di a dem	nu tri ment	va can cy	ar ro gant
di a lect	o ver plus	va gran cy	bar ris ter
dra per y	po et ry	ab do men	but ter y
droll e ry	pri ma cy	al le gro	ben e fit
du ti ful	pri ma ry	ad mi ral	big a my
flu en cy	pu ri ty	al co ran	big ot ry
i ro ny	re gen cy	an im al	but ter fly
i vo ry	ru di ment	an nu al	cal i co
la zi ness	se cre cy	ac ci dent	cal en dar
li bra ry	scru ti ny	al i ment	cab in et

c

can is ter	en ti ty	len i ty	ped i gree
can ni bal	ep i gram	lep ro sy	pen al ty
can o py	es cu lent	lev i ty	pen u ry
cap i tal	ev e ry	lib er al	pes ti lent
chast i ty	fac ul ty	lib er ty	pil lo ry
cin na mon	fac to ry	lig a ment	prac tic al
cit i zen	fam i ly	lin e al	prin cip al
clar i fy	fel o ny	lit a ny	pub lic an
clas sic al	fes tiv al	lit er al	punc tu al
clem en cy	fin ic al	lit ur gy	pun gen cy
cler ic al	fish er y	lux u ry	pyr a mid
cur ren cy	gal lant ry	man i fest	rad ic al
cyl in der	gal le ry	man i fold	rar i ty
den i zen	gar ri son	man ner ly	reg u lar
det ri ment	gen e ral	mar in er	rem e dy
dif fid ent	gun ner y	med ic al	rib ald ry
dif fer ent	hap pi ness	mel o dy	rev er end
dif fi cult	her ald ry	mem o ry	rit u al
dig ni ty	im ple ment	mes sen ger	riv u let
dil i gent	im pu dent	mil lin er	sac ra ment
div id end	in cre ment	min er al	sal a ry
dul cim er	in di go	min is ter	sat is fy
ec sta cy	in dus try	mus cu lar	sec u lar
ed it or	in fan cy	mys te ry	sed i ment
ef fi gy	in fant ry	nat u ral	sen a tor
el e ment	in fi del	pan o ply	sen ti ment
el e gy	in stru ment	par a dox	sen tin el
em bas sy	in te ger	par a gon	sev er al
eb o ny	in tel lect	par al lax	sil la bub
em bry o	in ter est	par al lel	sim il ar
em e rald	in ter val	par a pet	sin gu lar
em pe ror	in va lid	par i ty	sin is ter
en e my	jus ti fy	pat ri ot	slip pe ry
en mi ty	leg a cy	ped ant ry	sub si dy

sum ma ry	ur gen cy	hos pi tal	prod i gal
sup ple ment	wag gon er	lot te ry	prod i gy
sym me try	wil der ness	mon u ment	prom in ent
tam a rind	här bin ger	nem in al	prop er ty
tap es try	har mo ny	oc u kur	pros o dy
tem po ral	harps i chord	oc cu py	prot est ant
ten den cy	côd i cil	of fi cer	quad ru ped
ten e ment	col o ny	or a tor	qual i ty
ter ri fy	com e dy	or i gin	quan ti ty
tes ta ment	com ic al	or na ment	quan da ry
tit u lar	con ju gal	or re ry	cêr ti fy
typ ic al	con tin ent	ot to man	mer cu ry
tyr an ny	con tra band	pol i cy	per fi dy
vag a bond	con tra ry	pol i tic	per ju ry
van i ty	doc u ment	pop u lar	per ma nent
vic tor y	drop sic al	pov er ty	per tin ent
vil la ny	glob u lar	pon der ous	reg u late
vin e gar	gloss a ry	prob i ty	ter ma gaut

———⟶✳⟵———

TABLE VII.

Easy words of three syllables, accented on the second.

A bāse ment	de co rum	im pru dent
a gree ment	de ni al	oc ta vo
al li ance	de cri al	op po nent
al lure ment	de port ment	po ma tum
ap pa rent	de po nent	pri me val
ar ri val	dic ta tor	re ci tal
a maze ment	di plo ma	re li ance
a tone ment	en rol ment	re qui tal
co e qual	en tice ment	re vi val
con fine ment	e qua tor	spec ta tor
con trol ler	he ro ic	sub scri ber
de ci pher	il le gal	sur vi vor

tes ta tor	di min ish	pro tect or
tes ta trix	dis sent er	pu is sant
trans la tor	dis tem per	re dund ant
trans pa rent	dis tin guish	re fresh ment
tri bu nal	di ur nal	re lin quish
ver ba tim	dog mat ic	re luc tant
vol ca no	do mes tic	re mem ber
un e qual	dra mat ic	re plen ish
un mind ful	e ject ment	re plev in
a ban don	em bar rass	re pug nant
ac cus tom	em bel lish	re pub lish
af fect ed	em pan nel	ro man tic
ag gress or	en camp ment	se ques ter
a mend ment	e quip ment	spe cif ic
ap par el	er rat ic	sur ren der
ap pend ix	es tab lish	to bac co
as cend ant	hys ter ic	trans cend ent
as sas sin	in ces sant	trans gress or
as sem bly	in clem ent	tri umph ant
at tach ment	in cum bent	um brel la
at tend ant	in hab it	a bol ish
be gin ning	in sip id	ac com plish
be wil der	in trin sic	ad mon ish
co hab it	in val id	as ton ish
col lect or	ma lig nant	de mol ish
con sid er	mo nas tic	dis solv ent
con tin gent	noc tur nal	im mod est
con tract or	pa cif ic	im mor tal
de cant er	pe dant ic	im pos tor
de lin quent	po lem ic	im prop er
de liv er	pre cept or	in con stant
de mer it	pre tend er	in sol vent
de tach ment	pro hib it	im mor al
di lem ma	pro lif ic	un god ly

TABLE VIII.

Easy words of three syllables, accented on the first and third.

Al a móde	o ver take	in cor rect
dev o tee	rec on cile	in ter mix
dis a gree	ref u gee	o ver run
dis es teem	su per sede	o ver turn
dom i neer	su per scribe	rec ol lect
im ma ture	vol un teer	rec om mend
im por tune	un der mine	rep re hend
in com mode	ap pre hend	su per add
in ter cede	con de scend	un der stand
in tro duce	con tra dict	un der sell
mis ap ply	dis pos sess	dis con cern
mis be have	in di rect	dis con nect

———o*o———

TABLE IX.

Easy words of four syllables, the full accent on the first, and the half accent on the third.

Lù mi na ry	dil a to ry	preb end a ry
mo ment a ry	ep i lep sy	pref a to ry
au ga to ry	em is sa ry	pur ga to ry
bre vi a ry	ig no min y	sal u ta ry
ac cu ra cy	in ti ma cy	sanc tu a ry
ac ri mo ny	in tri ca cy	sec re ta ry
ad mi ral ty	in vent o ry	sed en ta ry
ad ver sa ry	man da to ry	stat u a ry
al i mo ny	mat ri mo ny	sump tu a ry
al le go ry	mer ce na ry	ter ri to ry
cer e mo ny	mis cel la ny	tes ti mo ny
cus tom a ry	mil i ta ry	trib u ta ry
del i ca cy	pat ri mo ny	per emp to ry
dif fi cul ty	plan et a ry	sub lu na ry

côn tro ver sy	prom on to ry	con tu ma cy
mon as te ry	vol un ta ry	con tu me ly
ob sti na cy	ob du ra cy	drom e da ry
prom is so ry	com ment a ry	com mis sa ry

The words het-e-ro-dox, lin-e-a-ment, pat-ri-ot-ism, sep-tu-a-gint, have the full accent on the first syllable, and the half accent on the last.

TABLE X.

Easy words of four syllables, accented on the second.

A e ri al	ob scu ri ty	cap tiv i ty
an nu i ty	ob tain a ble	ce lib a cy
ar mo ri al	pro pri e ty	ci vil i ty
cen tu ri on	se cu ri ty	cli mac ter ic
col le gi al	so bri e ty	co in cid ent
com mu nic ant	va cu i ty	col lat e ral
com mu ni ty	va ri e ty	com par is on
con gru i ty	ab surd i ty	com pet it or
con nu bi al	ac tiv i ty	com pul so ry
cor po re al	ac cess a ry	con jec tur al
cre du li ty	ac cess o ry	con spir a cy
cri te ri on	ad min is ter	con stit u ent
e le gi ac	ad vers i ty	de cliv i ty
fu tu ri ty	a dul te ry	de lin quen cy
gram ma ri an	af fin i ty	de prav i ty
gra tu i ty	a nal o gy	di am e ter
his to ri an	a nat o my	dis par i ty
li bra ri an	an tag o nist	di vin i ty
ma te ri al	ar til le ry	ef fect u al
ma tu ri ty	a vid i ty	e lec tric al
me mo ri al	bar bar i ty	em pyr e al
mer cu ri al	bru tal i ty	e pis co pal
out rage ous ly	ca lam i ty	e pit o me

e quiv a lent	no bil i ty	ve nal i ty
e quiv o cal	nu mer ic al	vi cin i ty
e van gel ist	om nip o tent	a pol o gy
e vent u al	par tic u lar	a pos ta cy
fa tal i ty	per pet u al	as trol o gy
fer til i ty	po lit ic al	as tron o my
fes tiv i ty	po lyg a my	bi og ra phy
fi del i ty	pos ter i ty	com mod i ty
for mal i ty	pre cip'it ant	con com it ant
fru gal i ty	pre dic a ment	de moc ra cy
gram mat ic al	pro fund i ty	de spond en cy
ha bit u al	pros per i ty	e con o my
hos til i ty	ra pid i ty	ge om e try
hu man i ty	re cip ro cal	hy poc ri sy
hu mil i ty	re pub lic an	ma jor i ty
i den ti ty	sab bat ic al	me trop o lis
im mens i ty	sa tan ic al	mi nor i ty
im ped im ent	scur ril i ty	mo nop o ly
ju rid ic al	se ver i ty	pre dom in ate
le vit ic al	sig nif ic ant	pri or i ty
lon gev i ty	se ren i ty	tau tol o gy
ma lev o lent	sin cer i ty	ver bos i ty
ma lig ni ty	so lem ni ty	ad ver si ty
mil len ni um	su prem a cy	di ver si ty
mo ral i ty	ter res tri al	e ter ni ty
mu nif i cent	tran quil li ty	hy per bo le
na tiv i ty	ty ran nic al	pro verb i al
ne ces si ty	va lid i ty	sub serv i ent

TABLE XI.

Easy words of four syllables; the full accent on the third, and the half accent on the first.

An te cé dent	com ment a tor
ap par a tus	me di a tor

sa cer do tal	mem o ran dum
su per vi sor	o ri ent al
ac ci dènt al	or na ment al
ar o mat ic	pan e gyr ic
cal i man co	pred e ces sor
det ri ment al	sci en tif ic
en er get ic	sys tem at ic
fun da ment al	cor res pònd ent
in nu en do	hor i zon tal
mal e fac tor	u ni vèr sal
man i fes to	un der stand ing
at mos pher ic	o ver whelm ing

⁎ Having proceeded through tables, composed of easy words from one to four syllables, let the learner begin the following tables, which consist of more difficult words. In these the child will be much assisted by a knowledge of the figures and the use of the Italics.

If the instructor should think it useful to let his pupils read some of the easy lessons, before they have finished spelling, he may divide their studies—let them spell one part of the day, and read the other.

TABLE XII.

Difficult and irregular Monosyllables.

I would recommend this table to be read sometimes across the page.

Bày	clay	rail	flail	brain
day	way	frail	snail	chain
hay	ray	wail	laird	grain
lay	bray	mail	aid	slain
say	stray	nail	maid	train
may	slay	trail	stair	rain
pay	spay	bail	swear	main
pray	jail	ail	wear	plain
sway	pail	hail	bear	sprain
fray	sail	tail	tear	stain

twain	tray	change	squeal	creed
vain	gay	strange	beer	heed
wain	slay	blaze	peer	mead
paint	play	be	deer	knead
quaint	beard	pea	fear	reed
plaint	date	sea	dear	bleed
aim	tale	tea	hear	breed
claim	staid	flea	near	plead
main	laid	yea	rear	deem
waif	paid	key	veer	seem
stage	braid	leap	drear	cream
gauge	air	neap	clear	dream
plague	chair	reap	shear	stream
vague	fair	cheap	steer	beam
bait	hair	heap	bier	steam
great	pair	steel	tier	seam
gait	lain	kneel	year	gleam
wait	pain	teal	cheer	scream
plait	strain	feel	heard	fleam
strait	gain	keel	blear	fream
graze	blain	deal	ear	ream
praise	drain	heal	sear	team
raise	fain	meal	smear	least
baise	faint	peel	spear	feast
raze	taint	reel	tear	yeast
maize	saint	seal	queer	beast
shave	trait	steal	deed	priest
brave	haste	veal	feed	east
knave	paste	weal	need	reef
break	waste	zeal	weed	grief
steak	baste	peal	bead	brief
spray	chaste	beal	lead	chief
stay	taste	ceil	read	deaf
gray	traipse	eel	seed	leaf

sheaf	teat	sleeve	league	sleight
fief	beak	grieve	teague	bright
liet	leak	reeve	tweag	fight
beef	weak	leave	leash	blight
plea	bleak	lieve	liege	fright
flee	sneak	reave	siege	flight
bee	speak	beeves	dry	wight
deep	freak	eaves	bye	wright
keep	squeak	greaves	fly	clime
weep	reek	freeze	cry	rhyme
steep	cheek	sneeze	sky	knife
sleep	wreak	breeze	lie	climb
creep	fleak	ease	die	smile
sheep	screak	squeeze	eye	stile
fleece	shriek	cheese	buy	guile
peace	sleek	frieze	try	mild
cease	streak	please	fry	child
lease	seen	seize	pie	wild
geese	bean	tease	wry	bride
niece	clean	speech	high	stride
piece	mien	leach	nigh	guide
grease	queen	beach	sigh	guise
crease	wean	reach	by	fro
meet	keen	teach	fie	doe
bleat	glean	screech	hie	toe
cheat	spleen	breach	vie	foe
treat	dean	bleach	light	bow
meat	green	each	might	mow
seat	quean	peach	height	tow
feat	yean	fiend	night	row
beat	lean	yield	right	owe
neat	mean	shield	sight	flow
feet	heave	wield	tight	glow
heat	cleave	field	slight	blow

slow	roast	loan	hoarse	rue
know	coast	shown	source	shrew
grow	toast	old	coarse	spew
snow	more	told	board	stew
stow	four	cold	hoard	tew
strow	pour	mold	gourd	yew
dough	door	port	sword	chew
hoe	floor	ort	holme	clew
sloe	roar	sport	oaf	ewe
mole	boar	court	loaf	slue
pole	hoar	goad	due	mew
sole	oar	load	true	cure
foal	soar	toad	you	pure
goal	oat	woad	glue	your
roll	boat	soap	sue	rude
poll	doat	froze	dew	prude
boll	goat	close	few	shrewd
toll	moat	prose	new	crude
soul	bloat	chose	pew	feud
scroll	float	coach	lieu	rheum
coal	joke	poach	view	muse
shoal	oak	roach	flew	bruise
bowl	croak	brouch	grew	use
knoll	cloke	folks	screw	cruise
stroll	soak	coax	brew	spruce
troll	tone	foam	blew	use
brogue	own	roam	drew	juice
rogue	known	comb	knew	cruse
vogue	groan	loam	crew	sluice
most	blown	shorn	hew	fruit
post	flown	sworn	strew	bruit
host	mown	mourn	shew	suit
ghost	sown	force	slew	mewl
boast	moan	course	blue	lure

jamb	check	delve	skill	jolt
lamb	speck	valve	spill	boult
plaid	wreck	guess	chill	dolt
limb	meant	breast	ditch	moult
gaunt	sense	guest	pitch	coat
dense	tense	sweat	witch	dost
hence	bench	debt	twitch	curl
pence	clench	stem	niche	hurl
fence	stench	phlegm	hinge	churl
lapse	quench	wink	singe	drum
flat	wench	pink	cringe	dumb
gnat	wrench	cinque	fringe	crumb
cash	drench	prism	twinge	numb
clash	fetch	schism	glimpse	plum
gnash	sketch	chip	since	much
strap	wretch	skip	rince	such
wrap	spend	ship	wince	touch
shall	friend	strip	teint	crutch
bled	blend	scrip	brick	burst
dead	badge	spin	stick	stuff
stead	fadge	chin	kick	snuff
read	edge	twin	wick	rough
tread	hedge	skin	quick	tough
bread	wedge	guilt	spit	plump
dread	sledge	built	knit	stump
sqread	ledge	quilt	twit	trump
shred	sedge	build	live	lurch
head	pledge	drift	sieve	church
cleanse	dredge	shift	ridge	young
realm	fledge	swift	none	gulf
dram	bridge	twist	stone	nymph
deck	bilge	wrist	home	hymn
neck	helve	risk	bolt	judge
peck	twelve	shrill	colt	grudge

drudge	lost	sawn	squall	cough
trudge	tost	brawn	yawl	trough
shrub	war	spawn	awl	fork
scrub	fort†	yawn	haul	cork
bulge	nort†	laud	stall	hawk
gurge	taught	fraud	small	balk
surge	caught	broad	crawl	walk
purge	brought	cord	brawl	talk
plunge	sought	lord	bawl	chalk
curse	ought	ward	caul	stalk
purse	wrought	gauze	drawl	calk
law	fought	cause	wart	daub
shaw	groat	pause	sort	bawd
taw	fraught	clause	short	warp
maw	naught	torch	quart	wasp
raw	form	scorch	snort	want
paw	storm	gorge	bald	sause
saw	swarm	all	scald	bâlm
awe	warm	tall	off	calm
gnaw	born	fall	oft	palm
straw	corn	hall	loft	psalm
flaw	warn	gall	soft	qualm
draw	corse	pall	cross	alms
chaw	horn	ball	dross	bask
claw	morn	call	moss	cask
craw	fawn	wall	loss	ask
haw	lawn	maul	horse	mask
jaw	dawn	scrawl	corpse	task
cost*	pawn	sprawl	dwarf	ark

* Perhaps *o* and *a* in the words *cost, corn, warm,* &c. may be considered as coming more properly under the figure 5. But the liquids that follow them, have such an effect in lengthening the syllable, that it appears more natural to place them under figure 3. A similar remark applies to *a* in *bar.*

† These words, when unemphatical, are necessarily short.

D

bark	starve	daunt	gape	knock
dark	arm	flaunt	carn	drop
bark	harm	haunt	darn	crop
mark	charm	jaunt	barn	shop
lark	farm	taunt	yarn	shock
park	barm	vaunt	bar	wan
spark	art	cast	far	swan
arc	cart	past	scar	gone
shark	dart	last	spar	wash
stark	hart	vast	star	swash
asp	mart	blast	tar	watch
clasp	part	fast	czar	was
hasp	tart	mast	car	wast
rasp	start	mass	char	knob
gasp	smart	pass	jar	swab
grasp	chart	lass	mar	wad
hard	heart	bass	par	dodge
bard	staff	brass	barb	lodge
card	chaff	class	garb	bodge
lard	half	glass	carle	podge
guard	calf	grass	marl	fosse
pard	laugh	arch	snarl	bond
yard	craft	march	chance	fond
branch	shaft	parch	dance	pond
launch	waft	starch	prance	wand
staunch	raft	harsh	lance	strong
haunch	draught	charge	glance	wrong
blanch	aft	large	trance	botch
craunch	haft	barge	scarf	scotch
carp	pant	farce	laste	mosque
harp	grant	parse	swåp	blot
sharp	slant	calve	dock	yacht
scarp	ant	halve	mock	scoat
carve	aunt	salve	clock	halt

salt	spool	woo	roof	stirp
malt	droop	proof	loof	chirp
fault	scoop	woof	soon	jerk
vault	troop	loose	hoop†	perk
false	loop	goose	coop	smerk
bronze	soup	moose	poop	yerk
doom	group	spoon	full	quirk
room	hoop*	roost	pull	herb
boom	boot	root	pull	verb
loom	coot	foot	wool	fir
bloom	hoot	shoot	bush	myrrh
groom	toot	look	push	fern
womb	moot	cook	puss	earn
tomb	food	hook	earl	yearn
broom	rood	look	pearl	learn
spoon	brood	took	skirt‡	stern
boon	mood	brook	verse	kern
moon	move	crook	fierce	quern
noon	prove	flock	pierce	search
loon	groove	rook	tierce	perch
swoon	noose	shook	herse	swerve
bourn	choose	croup	terse	wert
poor	lose	wood	verge	son
tour	boose	stood	serge	run
moor	ooze	good	dirge	ton
boor	ouse	hood	virge	won
cool	coo	could	vert	done
fool	two	would	term	one§
tool	do	should	firm	come
stool	shoe	wolf	germ	some
pool	loo	hoof	sperm	bomb

* To cry out.   † Of a cask.
‡ Under this figure, in the words *skirt*, &c. i has the sound of second e.
§ Pronounced wun

ciomb	once*	foil	brow	browse
rhomb	monk	boil	plow	spouse
dirt	tongue	coil	bough	drowse
shirt	birch	join	slough	cloud
flirt	sponge	coin	out	crowd
wort	heir	loin	stout	loud
girt	trey	groin	oust	proud
spirt	sley	boy	trout	shroud
squirt	prey	joy	gout	bound
kirk	grey	toy	pout	hound
work	weigh	coy	clout	pound
bird	eigh	cloy	rout	round
word	neigh	buoy	shout	sound
first	reign	point	spout	ground
worst	vein	joint	scout	wound
worse	feign	voice	douit	foul
blood	deign	choice	bout	owl
flood	skein	moist	drought	fowl
sir	rein	hoist	our	scowl
her	eight	joist	sour	cowl
stir	freight	noise	brown	growl
worm	weight	quoit	crown	howl
world	streight	coif	down	bounce
front	tete	quoif	drown	ounce
ront	feint	ou and ow	frown	pounce
wont	veil	now	clown	flounce
dove	oi and oy	cow	gown	couch
love	oil	how	town	vouch
shove	spoil	bow	house	slouch
glove	soil	mow	louse	pouch
twirl	broil	sow	mouse	gouge
dunce	toil	vow	douse	lounge

* Pronounced wunce.

MONOSYLLABLES in *T'H.*

The following have the first sound of th, *viz. as in* thick, thin.

Throw	thowl	hath	breadth	bath
truth	threw	rath	filth	lath
youth	thrice	pith	frith	wrath
sheath	thrive	with*	plinth	thrôb
heath	throne	theft	spilth	throng
both	throe	thatch	thâw	thong
oath	throve	thill	cloth	tôoth
forth	thing	thrid	moth	through
fourth	think	thrill	broth	earth
highth	thin	thrush	sloth	dearth
three	thank	thwack	troth	bĩrth
throat	thick	tilth	north	girth
theme	thrift	withe	loth	mirth
thigh	thumb	doth	thought	third
thief	thump	smith	thorn	thirst
faith	length	thrust	froth	worth
blowth	strength	thrum	thrall	month
growth	breath	thread	thwart	thirl
quoth	death	stealth	warmth	*ou*
ruth	health	thrash	swath	south
teeth	wealth	depth	pâth	mouth
thane	threat	width	hearth	drouth

* In this word, *th* has its first sound before a consonant, as in *withstand;* and its second sound before a vowel, as in *without, with us.* But in other compound words, *th* generally retains the sound of its primitive.

The following have the second sound of th, *as in* thou.

Thine	teeth*	blithe	then	soothe
thy	those	wreath	thus	they
bathe	tithe	writhe	the	there
lathe	these	sythe	them	their
swathe	though	seethe	thence	ou
clothe	thee	breathe	than	thou
loathe	hithe	this	booth	mouth
meethe	lithe	that	smooth	

* The noun *teeth*, has the first sound of *th*, and the verb to *teeth*, its second sound. The same is observable of *mouth* and to *mouth* This is the reason why these words are found under both heads.

The words *mouth, moth, cloth, oath, path, sheath, bath, lath,* have the first sound of *th* in the singular number, and the second in the plural.

Examples of the formation of plurals, and other derivatives.

Bay,	bays	stain,	stains	saint,	saints
day,	days	brain,	brains	heap,	heaps
lay,	lays	chain,	chains	tear,	tears
pay,	pays	pain,	pains	hear,	hears
pray,	prays	paint,	paints	spear,	spears
sway,	sways	claim,	claims	creed,	creeds
way,	ways	strait,	straits	trait,	traits
mail,	mails	plague,	plagues	chief,	chiefs
nail,	nails	key,	keys	leak,	leaks
sail,	sails	knave,	knaves	speak,	speaks
weep,	weeps	green,	greens	sheaf,	sheaves
seam,	seams	yield,	yields	leaf,	leaves
fly,	flies	stride,	strides	poll,	polls
cry,	cries	guide,	guides	soul,	souls
dry,	dries	smile,	smiles	coal,	coals

sky,	skies	toe,	toes	bowl,	bowls
buy,	buys	foe,	foes	rogue,	rogues
sigh,	sighs	bow,	bows	post,	posts
flight,	flights	glow,	glows	host,	hosts
light,	lights	flow,	flows	toast,	toasts
sight,	sights	blow,	blows	coast,	coasts
life,	lives	snow,	snows	door,	doors
wife,	wives	hoe,	hoes	floor,	floors
knife,	knives	foal,	foals	oar,	oars

TABLE XIII.

Lessons of easy words, to teach children to read, and to know their duty.

LESSON I.

No man may put off the law of God:
My joy is in his law all the day.
O may I not go in the way of sin!
Let me not go in the way of ill men.

II.

A bad man is a foe to the law;
It is his joy to do ill.
All men go out of the way.
Who can say he has no sin?

III.

The way of man is ill.
My son, do as you are bid:
But if you are bid, do no ill.
See not my sin, and let me not go to the pit.

IV.

Rest in the Lord, and mind his word.
My son, hold fast the law that is good.
You must not tell a fie, nor do hurt.
We must let no man hurt us.

V.

Do as well as you can, and do no harm.
Mark the man that doth well, and do so too.
Help such as want help, and be kind.
Let your sins past put you in mind to mend.

VI.

I will not walk with bad men, that I may not
      be cast off with them.
I will love the law and keep it.
I will walk with the just and do good.

VII.

This life is not long; but the life to come has
     no end.
We must pray for them that hate us.
We must love them that love not us.
We must do as we like to be done to.

VIII.

A bad life will make a bad end.
He must live well that will die well.
He doth live ill that doth not mend.
In time to come we must do no ill.

IX.

No man can say that he has done no ill,
For all men have gone out of the way.
There is none that doth good; no, not one.
If I have done harm, I must do it no more.

X.

Sin will lead us to pain and woe.
Love that which is good, and shun vice.
Hate no man, but love both friends and foes.
A bad man can take no rest, day nor night.

XI.

He who came to save us, will wash us from all sin: I will be glad in his name.

A good boy will do all that is just; he will flee from vice; he will do good, and walk in the way of life.

Love not the world, nor the things that are in the world; for they are sin.

I will not fear what flesh can do to me; for my trust is in him who made the world:

He is nigh to them that pray to him, and praise his name.

XII.

Be a good child; mind your book; love your school, and strive to learn.

Tell no tales; call no ill names; you must not lie, nor swear, nor cheat, nor steal.

Play not with bad boys; use no ill words at play; spend your time well; live in peace, and shun all strife. This is the way to make good men love you, and save your soul from pain and woe.

XIII.

A good child will not lie, swear, nor steal. —He will be good at home, and ask to read his book; when he gets up he will wash his hands and face clean; he will comb his hair, and make haste to school; he will not play by the way, as bad boys do.

XIV.

When good boys and girls are at school, they will mind their books, and try to learn to spell and read well, and not play in the time of school.

When they are at church, they will sit, kneel, or stand still; and when they are at home, will read some good book, that God may bless them.

XV.

As for those boys and girls that mind not their books, and love not the church and school, but play with such as tell tales, tell lies, curse, swear, and steal, they will come to some bad end, and must be whipt till they mend their ways.

---◦✳◦---

TABLE XVI.

Words of two syllables accented on the first.

1	sea ture	ni ter	tai lor
A cre	fe male	oat meal	trai tor
a pron	fro ward	past ry	trea ty
bare foot	grate ful	pi ous	wea ry
beast ly	griev ous	peo ple	wo ful
brew er	gno mon	plu mage	wri ter
beau ty	hein ous	pa rent	wain scot
brok en	hind most	pro logue	yeo man
boat swain	hoar y	quo ta	ab sence
bow sprit	hu mor	rhu barb	ab bey
brave ry	jew el	ri fle	am ple
ca ble	jui cy	rogu ish	asth ma
cheap en	knave ry	re gion	an cle
dai ly	knight hood	sea son	bal ance
dai sy	li ver	spright ly	bel fry
dea con	la bor	sti fle	bash ful
dia mond	le gion	stee ple	bish op
do tage	may or	bol ster	blem ish
eve ning	me ter	coul ter	blus ter
fa vor	mi ter	slave ry	brim stone
fla vor	mea sles	shoul der	brick kiln

blud geon	dam son	grav el	mel on
bel lows	dan gle	grum ble	mer it
bis cuit	dac tyl	guin ea	min gle
brit tle	debt or	guin ea	mis tress
buck ram	dim ple	gud geon	mis chief
bus tle	dis tance	hand ful	musk et
cam el	doub le	hab it	mus lin
cap rice	driv en	has soc	mus ter
cap tain	dud geon	hav oc	mar riage
cen sure	dun geon	heif er	nev er
chap el	drunk ard	heav y	nim ble
chas ten	dust y	hin drance	pad lock
cher ish	ec logue	hus band	pamph let
chim ney	en gine	hum ble	pen ance
car ry	en sign	husk y	pes ter
car riage	en trails	im age	phren zy
cis tern	er ror	in stance	pis mire
cit y	fash ion	in ward	plan et
clam or	fam ish	isth mus	pleas ant
clean ly	fas set	jeal ous	peas ant
cred it	fat ten	jour nal	pinch ers
crev ice	fes ter	judge ment	prat tle
crick et	fer riage	knuck le	pun ish
crust y	fid dle	knap sack	puz zle
crys tal	flag on	lan guage	pic ture
cup board	free kle	lan guor	pur chase
cus tom	frus trate	land lord	prac tice
crib bage	fur lough	lev el	phthis ic
cul ture	fran chise	lim it	punch eon
cous in	ges ture	lus ter	quick en
cut lass	gant let	lunch eon	ram ble
dam age	gin gle	mad am	rap id
dam ask	glis ten	mal ice	rat tle
dam sel	grand eur	man gle	reb el
		mas tiff	

rel ish	tav ern	daugh ter	mark et
rig or	tempt er	au tumn	mas ter
ris en	ten ant	fault y	mar quis
riv er	till age	for tress	par cel
riv et	tip ple	for tune	par don
ruf fle	tress pass	gau dy	par lor
res in	troub le	geor gic	part ner
sam ple	twink ling	gorge ous	pas ture
salm on	trans port	lau rel	psalm ist
satch el	trun cheon	lord ship	scar let
scab bard	ven om	haugh ty	slan der
scis sors	ven ture	morn ing	ål so
seven night	vint age	mor tal	al way
scep ter	vis it	mort gage	bon fire
spec ter	vis age	naugh ty	cob ler
scrib ble	vict uals	saw yer	clos et
scuf fle	venge ance	tor ment	col league
sin ew	veni son	wa ter	com et
sim ple	vine yard	sau cy	com rade
sin gle	wel come	sau cer	con quer
scep tic	wed lock	ân swer	cock swain
smug gle	wick ed	barb er	con duit
span gle	wran gle	brace let	cop y
spig ot	wrap per	cart er	con trite
spit tle	wres tle	cham ber	cof fin
spin dle	wrist band	craft y	doc trine
sup ple	weap on	char coal	flor id
subt le	wid geon	flask et	fon dle
stur geon	zeal ot	gar land	fore head
sur geon	zeal ous	ghast ly	frol ic
tal ent	zeph yr	gar ment	fal chion
tal on	slaugh ter	har lot	grog ram
tan gle	bor der	har vest	gos lin
tat tle	cor ner	jaun dice	hogs head

hom age	spon dee	coop er	shov el
hon est	wan der	cuck oo	squir rel
hon or	wan ton	vêr min	vir gin
knowl edge	war rant	ver dict	wor ship
hal loe	squan der	ver juice	won der
lodg er	yon der	vir tue	nêigh bor
mod est	gloôm y	kern el	ou
mod ern	wo man	côn jure	coun cil
mon strous	boo by	cov er	coun ter
nov el	wôol len	cir cuit	coun ty
nov ice	bush el	fir kin	dough ty
prof fer	bo som	com pass	drow sy
prog ress	bush y	com fort	mount ain
prom ise	worst ed	bor ough	show er
pros pect	cush ion	dirt y	flow er
pros per	bul let	gov ern	bow er
quad rant	bul lock	hon ey	pow er
quad rate	bul ly	sove reign	oy
squad ron	bul wark	stir rup	voy age
stop page	butch er	skir mish	

TABLE XV.

Lesson I.

THE time will come when we must all be laid in the dust.

Keep thy tongue from ill, and thy lips from guile. Let thy words be plain and true to the thoughts of the heart.

He that strives to vex or hurt those that sit next him, is a bad boy, and will meet with foes let him go where he will: but he that is kind, and loves to live in peace, will make friends of all that know him.

E

A clown will not make a bow, nor thank you when you give him what he wants; but he that is well bred will do both.

He that speaks loud in school will not learn his own book well, nor let the rest learn theirs; but those that make no noise will soon be wise, and gain much love and good will.

II.

Shun the boy that tells lies, or speaks bad words; for he would soon bring thee to shame.

He that does no harm shall gain the love of the whole school; but he that strives to hurt the rest, shall gain their ill will.

He that lies in bed when he should go to school, is not wise; but he that shakes off sleep shall have praise.

He is a fool that does not choose the best boys when he goes to play; for bad boys will cheat, and lie, and swear, and strive to make him as bad as themselves.

Slight no man for you know not how soon you may stand in need of his help.

III.

If you have done wrong, own your fault; for he that tells a lie to hide it, makes it worse.

He that tells the truth is a wise child; but he that tells lies, will not be heard when he speaks the truth.

When you are at school, make no noise, but keep your seat, and mind your book; for what you learn will do you good, when you grow to be a man

Play no tricks on them that sit next you; for

if you do, good boys will shun you as they would a dog that they knew would bite them.

He that hurts you at the same time that he calls you his friend, is worse than a snake in the grass.

Be kind to all men, and hurt not thyself.

A wise child loves to learn his book, but the fool would choose to play with toys.

IV.

Sloth keeps such a hold of some boys, that they lie in bed when they should go to school; but a boy that wants to be wise will drive sleep far from him.

Love him that loves his book, and speaks good words, and does no harm: For such a friend may do thee good all the days of thy life.

Be kind to all as far as you can; you know not how soon you may want their help; and he that has the good will of all that know him, shall not want a friend in time of need.

If you want to be good, wise, and strong, read with care such books as have been made by wise and good men; think of what you read in your spare hours; be brisk at play, but do not swear; and waste not too much of your time in bed.

TABLE XVI.

Words of two syllables, accented on the second.

Ac quire	af fair	ap proach	a stray
a base	af fright	ar raign	a vail
a buse	a gainst	a rise	a wake
a dieu	a muse	as sign	a way

al ly	en croach	un tie	a far
aw ry	en dear	un true	a larm
be lieve	en treat	up right	guit ar
be lief	ex cise	ad journ	in graft
be nign	ex pose	a byss	re mark
be siege	in crease	at tack	sur pass
be low	in dict	at tempt	ca tarrh
be stow	im pair	a venge	re gard
bo hea	in fuse	ad ept	ap prove
con sign	in scribe	be head	a mour
com plain	ma lign	be twixt	bab oon
cam paign	ob tain	bur lesque	bas soon
com pose	o pake	con temn	be hoove
con dign	ob lige	con tempt	buf foon
con cise	per tain	co quet	ca noe
con ceit	pre vail	e nough	car touch
con fuse	pre scribe	fi nesse	dis prove
con strain	pro pose	ga zette	a do
de ceive	pur suit	gro tesque	a loof
de ceit	pro rogue	har angue	e merge
de crease	re ceive	im mense	im merse
de light	re ceipt	qua drille	af firm
de pose	re course	so journ	de sert
de scribe	re pair	be cause	de serve
de sign	re pose	a dorn	a bove
de sire	re prieve	a broad	a mong
de vise	re straint	de fraud	be come
dis claim	re sume	de bauch	be love
dis course	re tain	per form	con vey
dis may	re sign	re ward	sur vey
dis own	sup pose	sub orn	in veigh
dis play	tran scribe	trans form	*oi*
dis pose	trans pose	e clat	ap point
in close	un close	ad vance	a noin.

a void	re joice	com pound	pro pound
em broil	sub join	con found	sur mount
en joy	dis joint	de vour	al low
de stroy	*ou*	ac count	a bound
de coy	a mount	pro nounce	an nounce
pur loin	a bout	re nounce	ca rouse

---◇*◇---

TABLE XVII.

Examples of words derived from their roots or primitives.

EXAMPLE I.

Prim.	Deriv.	Prim.	Deriv.	Prim.	Deriv.
Rain,	rain-y	grass,	grass-y	froth,	froth-y
rust,	rust-y	glass,	glass-y	drouth,	drouth-y
leaf.	leaf-y	ice,	i-cy	size,	si-zy
stick,	stick-y	frost,	frost-y	chill,	chill-y
pith,	pith-y	snow,	snow-y	chalk,	chalk-y
length,	length-y	fog,	fog-gy	down,	down-y
slight,	slight-y	wood,	wood-y	gloss,	gloss-y
storm,	storm-y	room,	room-y	worth,	wor-thy

EXAMPLE II.

Plural nouns of two syllables, formed from the singular of one syllable.

lace,	la-ces	brush,	brush-es	house,	hous-es
face,	fa-ces	price,	pri-ces	church,	church-es
pace,	pa-ces	slice,	sli-ces	box,	box-es
trace,	tra-ces	spice,	spi-ces	tierce,	tier-ces
cage,	ca-ges	grace,	gra-ces	verse,	vers-es
page,	pa-ges	press,	press-es	lodge,	lodg-es
nose,	no-ses	dress,	dress-es	watch,	watch-es
rose,	ro-ses	maze,	ma-zes	noise,	nois-es
curse,	curs-es	fish,	fish-es	voice,	voic-es
purse,	purs-es	horse,	hors-es	charge,	charg-es
surge,	surg-es	corps,	corps-es	sense,	sens-es

E 2

loss,	loss-es	cause,	caus-es	fringe,	frin-ges
arch,	arch-es	farce,	far-ces	ridge,	ridg-es
cheese,	chees-es	course,	cours-es	dance,	dan-ces

Example III.

Words formed by adding ing to verbs, and called Participles.

call,	call-ing	al-lay,	al-lay-ing
air,	air-ing	com-plain,	com-plain-ing
faint,	faint-ing	al-low,	al-low-ing
feel,	feel-ing	fin-ish,	fin-ish-ing
see,	see-ing	lav-ish,	lav-ish-ing
beat,	beat-ing	glim-mer,	glim-mer-ing

Words in which e final is omitted in the derivative.

change,	chang-ing	ex-change,	ex-chang-ing
glance,	glanc-ing	dis-pose,	dis-pos-ing
prance,	pranc-ing	gen-er-ate,	gen-e-rat-ing
grace,	grac-ing	con-verse,	con-vers-ing
give,	giv-ing	con-vince,	con-vin-cing
hedge,	hedg-ing	op-e-rate,	op-e-rat-ing
style,	styl-ing	dis-solve,	dis-solv-ing
solve,	solv-ing	im-i-tate,	im-i-tat-ing
tri-fle,	tri-fling	re-ceive,	re-ceiv-ing
ri-fle,	ri-fling	per-ceive,	per-ceiv-ing
shuf-fle,	shuf-fling	prac-tice,	prac-tic-ing

Example IV.

The manner of expressing degrees of comparison in qualities, by adding *er* and *est*, or *r* and *st*; called Positive, Comparative, and Superlative.

Pos.	Comp.	Superl.	Pos.	Comp.	Superl.
great,	great-er,	great-est	wise,	wis-er,	wis-est
kind,	kind-er,	kind-est	ripe,	rip-er,	rip-est
bold,	bold-er,	bold-est	rare,	rar-er,	rar-est
rich,	rich-er,	rich-est	grave,	grav-er,	grav-est
near,	near-er,	near-est	chaste,	chast-er,	chast-est
cold,	cold-er,	cold-est	brave,	brav-er,	brav-est
warm,	warm-er,	warm-est	vile,	vil-er,	vil-est

EXAMPLE V.

Words ending in *ish*, expressing a degree of quality less than the positive.

red-dish,	red,	red-der,	red-dest
brown-ish,	brown,	brown-er,	brown-est
whi-tish,	white,	whi-ter,	whit-est
green-ish,	green,	green-er,	green-est
black-ish,	black,	black-er,	black-est
blu-ish,	blue,	blu-er,	blu-est
yel-low-ish,	yel-low,	yel-low-er,	yel-low-est

EXAMPLE VI.

Formation of verbs in the three persons.

Present Time.

Singular number.			Plural.
1	2	3	
I love,	thou lovest, you love,	{ he loveth, he loves, she loves. it loves,	1 We love 2 ye *or* you love 3 they love
I grant,	thou grantest, you grant,	{ he granteth, he grants, she grants, it grants,	We grant ye *or* you grant they grant

Past Time.

I loved,	thou lovedst, you loved,	{ he loved, she loved, it loved,	We loved ye *or* you loved they loved

———✳———

TABLE XVIII.

Familiar Lessons.

A dog growls and barks; a cat mews and purrs; a cock crows; a hen clucks and cackles; a bird chirps and sings; an ox lows; a bull bellows; a lion roars; a horse neighs; an ass brays; a whale spouts. Birds fly in the air by the help of wings; snakes crawl on the earth without feet; fishes swim in water, by means of fins; beasts have feet, with hoofs or claws, to walk or run on land.

All animals are fitted for certain modes of living. The birds which feed on flesh, have strong claws, to catch and hold small animals, and a hooked bill to tear the flesh to pieces: such is the vulture and the hawk. Fowls which feed on insects and grain, have mostly a short straight bill, like the robin. Those which live on fish, have long legs for wading, or long bills for seizing and holding their prey, like the heron and the fish hawk. Fowls which delight chiefly to fly in the air, and light and build nests on the trees, have their toes divided, by which they cling to the branches and twigs; those which live in and about water have webbed feet, that is, their toes united by a film or skin, so that their feet serve as oars or paddles for swimming.

See the dog, the cat, the wolf, the lion, the panther and catamount; what sharp claws and pointed teeth they have, to seize little animals, and tear them in pieces! But see the gentle cow and ox, and timid sheep—these useful animals are made for man,—they have no claws, nor sharp teeth,—they have only blunt teeth in the under jaw, fitted to crop the grass of the field:—they feed in quiet, and come at the call of man. Oxen submit to the yoke, and plow the field, or draw the cart:—the cow returns home at evening, to fill the farmer's pails with milk, the wholesome food of men:—and the sheep yields her yearly fleece, to furnish us with warm garments.

Henry, tell me the number of days in a year. Three hundred and sixty-five.—How many weeks in a year? Fifty-two.—How many days in a week? Seven.—What are they called? Sunday, Monday, Tuesday, Wednesday, Thursday, Friday, Saturday: Sunday is the Sabbath, or day of rest, and called the Lord's day, being devoted to religious duties.—How many hours are there in a day? Twenty-four—How many minutes in an hour? Sixty, and sixty seconds in a minute. Time is measured by clocks and watches, dials and glasses. The light of the sun makes the day, and the shade of the earth makes the night. The earth is round, and rolls round from west to east once in twenty-four hours. The day time is for labor, and the night for sleep and repose. Children should go to bed early.

Charles, how is the year divided? Into months and seasons.——How many are the months? Twelve calendar months, and nearly thirteen lunar months. What are the names of the calendar months? January, February, March, April, May, June, July, August, September, October, November, December. January begins the year, and the first day of that month is called New Year's day. Then people express to each other their good wishes, and little boys and girls expect gifts of little books, toys and plums.—What is the lunar month? It is the time from one change of the moon to another, which is about twenty-nine days; and a half.

John, what are the seasons? Spring, summer, autumn or fall, and winter. The spring is so called from the springing or first shooting of the plants: when they put forth leaves and blossoms, all nature is decked with bloom, and perfumed with fragrant odors. The spring months are March, April, and May. The summer months are June, July, and August, when the sun pours his heating rays on the earth, the trees are clothed with leaves and fruit; and the ground is covered with herbage. The autumnal months are September, October, and November; which are also called *fall,* from the fall of the leaves. Now the fruits are gathered, the verdure of the plants decays; the leaves of the forest turn red or yellow, and fall from the trees, and nature is stripped of her verdant robes. Then comes dreary winter. In December, January, and February, frost binds the earth in chains, and spreads an icy bridge over rivers and lakes: the snow, with her white mantle, enwraps the earth; no birds fill the air with the music of their notes; the beasts stand shivering in the stall; and men crowd around the fire-side, or wrapped in wool and fur, prepare to meet the chilling blast.

ADVICE.

Prefer solid sense to vain wit; study to be useful rather than diverting; commend and respect nothing so much as true piety and virtue—Let no jest intrude to violate good manners; never utter what may offend the chastest ear.

TABLE XIX.

Words of three syllables, the full accent on the first, and the half accent on the third.

Note. In half accented terminations, *ate, ude, ure, ize, ule, ise, ule, uge, ide,* the vowel has its first sound generally, though not dwelt upon so long, or pronounced with so much force as in the full accented syllables. But in the terminations *ice, ive, ile,* the vowel has generally its second sound, and the final *e* is superfluous, or only softens *c;* as *notice, relative, juvenile,*—pronounced *notis, relativ, juvenil.* In the former case, the final *e* is in Roman; and in the latter case, in Italic.

Di a phragm	pleu ri sy	nam or ous
du pli cate	qui et ude	an ec dote
di a logue	rheu ma tism	an ti quate
aid de camp	ru min ate	ap ti tude
e go tism	scru pu lous	an o dyne
fa vor ite	se ri ous	ap er ture
for ci ble	spu ri ous	as y lum
fre quen cy	su i cide	bev e rage
fu gi tive	suit a ble	blun der buss
fea si ble	va ri ous	cat a logue
glo ri ous	u ni form	cal cu late
he ro ism	u su ry	can did ate
ju bi lee	ad jec tive	can dle stick
ju ve nile	ag gra vate	car a way
live li hood	an a pest	cel e brate
lu bri cate	an im ate	crit i cism
lu cra tive	ap pe tite	cim e tar
lu dic rous	al ti tude	court e sy
lu min ous	ab di cate	cul tiv ate
night in gale	ac cu rate	dec a logue
nu mer ous	ad e quate	dec o rate
o di ous	ac tu ate	ded ic ate
pre vi ous	ag o nize	def in ite
pa gan ism	al ge bra	del e gate

dem on strate	im pi ous	pen te cost
der o gate	in fa mous	per quis ite
des o late	in stig ate	phys ic al
des po tism	in sti tute	plen i tude
des pe rate	in tim ate	pres byt er
des ti tute	jeal ous y	pres id ent
dem a gogue	jeop ar dy	pris on er
ep au lette	jes sa mine	priv i lege
ep i logue	las si tude	quer u lous
el o quence	lat i tude	par a sol
el e vate	lib er tine	ral le ry
em pha sis	lit ig ate	ran cor ous
em u lous	mack er el	rap tur ous
en ter prize	mag ni tude	rav en ous
en vi ous	man u script	rec ti tude
ep i cure	mas sa cre	rel a tive
es tim ate	med i cine	ren o vate
ex cel lence	med it ate	re quis ite
fas cin ate	mis chiev ous	ren dez vous
fab u lous	met a phor	rep ro bate
feb ri fuge	musk mel on	res i dence
fluc tu ate	nour ish ment	res i due
fur be low	ped a gogue	ret i nue
gen er ous	pal li ate	rev er ence
gen tle man	pal pa ble	rev er end
gen u ine	pal pit ate	rhap so dy
grad u ate	par a ble	rhet o ric
gran a ry	par a dise	rid i cule
hem i sphere	par a digm	sac ri fice
hes it ate	par a phrase	sac ri lege
hand ker chief	par a site	sal iv ate
hur ri cane	par ent age	sas sa fras
hyp o crite	par ox ism	sat ir ize
im age ry	par ri cide	scav en ger

sens i ble	lau da ble	crock e ry
sep a rate	plau si ble	hor i zon
ser a phim	por phy ry	lon gi tude
stadt hold er	arch i tect	nom in ate
stim u late	ar gu ment	ob lig ate
stip u late	ar ma ment	ob lo quy
stren u ous	ar ti fice	ob sta cle
sub ju gate	bay o net	ob stin ate
sub se quent	bar ba rism	ob vi ous
sub sti tute	bar ba rous	om in ous
syn a gogue	car din al	op e rate
sim i le	car pen ter	op po site
scep ti cism	chan cel lor	or i fice
syn co pe	chan ce ry	prob a ble
sur ro gate	guar di an	pop u lous
syc o phant	ghast li ness	pos i tive
syl lo gism	lar ce ny	pot en tate
tan ta lize	mar gin al	prof li gate
tan ta mount	mas quer ade	proph e cy
tel e scope	par ti san	quar an tine
ten a ble	phar ma cy	pros e cute
tim o rous	par lia ment	por rin ger
treach er ous	rasp ber ry	pros per ous
trip lic ate	al der man	pros ti tute
tur pi tude	al ma nac	sol e cism
vas sal age	bot a ny	sol i tude
vin dic ate	col lo quy	soph is try
bil let doux	com pli ment	vol a tile
fraud u lent	com plai sance	roq ue laur
cor di al	con sti tute	tom a hawk
cor po ral	con tem plate	per se cute
for feit ure	com pen sate	per son age
for ti tude	con fis cate	prin ci ple
for tu nate	cor o ner	ser vi tude

F

ter min ate	com pa ny	roy al ty
firm a ment	come li ness	*ou*
mir a cle	gov ern or	coun sel lor
cir cu lar	gov ern ess	coun ter feit
cir cum stance	*oi*	coun te nance
cir cum spect	poig nan cy	boun ti ful

TABLE XX.

LESSON I.

My son, hear the counsel of thy father, and forsake not the law of thy mother.

If sinners entice thee to sin, consent thou not.

Walk not in the way with them; refrain thy feet from their path, for their feet run to evil, and make haste to shed blood.

II.

Be not wise in thine own eyes; but be humble.

Let truth only proceed from thy mouth.—Despise not the poor, because he is poor; but honor him who is honest and just. Envy not the rich, but be content with thy fortune. Follow peace with all men, and let wisdom direct thy steps.

III.

Happy is the man that findeth wisdom. She is of more value than rubies. Length of days is in her right hand, and in her left hand, riches and honor. Her ways are pleasant, and all her paths are peace. Exalt her and she shall promote thee: She shall bring thee to honor, when thou dost embrace her.

IV.

The ways of virtue are pleasant, and lead to life; but they who hate wisdom, love death. Therefore pursue the paths of virtue and peace, then safety and glory will be thy reward. All my delight is upon the saints that are in the earth, and upon such as excel in virtue.

TABLE XXI.

Words of three syllables, accented on the second.

A chiev ment	con jec ture	mis pris on
ac quaint ance	con vuls ive	pneu mat ics
ap prais er	de ben ture	pre sump tive
ar rear age	de fect ive	pro duc tive
blas phe mer	dis cour age	pro gres sive
con ta gion	dis par age	re puls ive
con ta gious	dis sem ble	re ten tive
cor ro sive	ef ful gent	re venge ful
cour age ous	en tan gle	rheu mat ic
de ceit ful	ex cul pate	stu pend ous
de ci sive	gym nas tic	sub mis sive
dif fu sive	ef fect ive	ab ôr tive
in qui ry	em bez zle	in dorse ment
e gre gious	en deav or	im port ance
en light en	ex cess ive	im pos ture
o bei sance	ex pens ive	per form ance
out rage ous	ex press ive	re cord er
pro ce dure	ex tens ive	mis for tune
po ta toe	ex cheq uer	ad vân tage
so no rous	es cutch eon	a part ment
mus ke toe	ho san na	de part ment
a bridge ment	il lus trate	dis as ter
ac knowl edge	i am bus	em bar go
ad ven ture	in cen tive	a pôs tle
af fran chise	in cul cate	re mon strate
ag grand ize	in dent ure	sub al tern
dis fran chise	in jus tice	ac côu ter
ap pren tice	in vec tive	ma neu ver
au tum nal	lieu ten ant	al têrn ate
bis sex tile	mo ment ous	de ter mine
com pul sive	of fens ive	re hears al
cur mud geon	op press ive	sub vers ive

The following are accented on the first and third
syllables.

Ap per tâin	con nois seur	em bra sure
ad ver tise	dis ap pear	ac qui êsce
as cer tain	en ter tain	co a lesce
con tra vene	gaz et teer	male con tent
can non ade	deb o nair	coun ter mând

———o*o———

TABLE XXII.

Words not exceeding three syllables, divided.

LESSON I.

THE wick-ed flee when no man pur-su-eth; but the right-e-ous are as bold as a li-on.

Vir-tue ex-alt-eth a na-tion; but sin is a re-proach to a-ny peo-ple.

The law of the wise is a foun-tain of life to de-part from the snares of death.

Wealth got-ten by de-ceit, is soon wast-ed; but he that gath-er-eth by la-bor, shall in-crease in rich-es.

II.

I-dle-ness will bring thee to pov-er-ty; but by in-dus-try and pru-dence thou shalt be fill-ed with bread.

Wealth mak-eth ma-ny friends; but the poor are for-got-ten by their neigh-bors.

A pru-dent man fore-seeth the e-vil, and hid-eth him-self; but the thought-less pass on and are pun-ish-ed.

III.

Train up a child in the way he should go, and when he is old he will not de-part from it.

Where there is no wood the fire go-eth out, and where there is no tat-ler the strife ceas-eth.

A word fit-ly spok-en is like ap-ples of gold in pic-tures of sil-ver.

He that cov-er-eth his sins shall not pros-per, but he that con-fess-eth and for-sak-eth them shall find mer-cy.

IV.

The rod and re-proof give wis-dom; but a child left to him-self bring-eth his pa-rents to shame.

Cor-rect thy son, and he will give thee rest; yea, he will give de-light to thy soul.

A man's pride shall bring him low; but hon-or shall up-hold the hum-ble in spir-it.

The eye that mock-eth at his fath-er, and scorn-eth to o-bey his moth-er, the ra-vens of the val-ley shall pick it out, and the young ea-gles shall eat it.

V.

By the bless-ing of the up-right, the cit-y is ex-alt-ed, but it is o-ver-thrown by the mouth of the wick-ed.

Where no coun-sel is, the peo-ple fall; but in the midst of coun-sel-lors there is safe-ty.

The wis-dom of the pru-dent is to un-der-stand his way, but the fol-ly of fools is de-ceit.

A wise man fear-eth and de-part-eth from evil, but the fool rag-eth and is con-fi-dent.

Be not hast-y in thy spir-it to be an-gry; for an-ger rest-eth in the bo-som of fools.

───◦◦◦◦❋◦◦◦◦───

TABLE XXIII.

Words of four syllables, accented on the first.

2	des pi ca ble	mis er a ble
Ad mi ra ble	el i gi ble	nav i ga ble
ac cu rate ly	es ti ma ble	pal li a tive
am i ca ble	ex pli ca tive	pit i a ble
ap pli ca ble	fig u ra tive	pref er a ble
ar ro gant ly	lam ent a ble	ref er a ble
cred it a ble	lit er a ture	rev o ca ble
crim in al ly	mar riage a ble	sump tu ous ly

F 2

spec u la tive   à mi a ble   cŏm mon al ty
suf fer a ble   ju di ca ture   nom in a tive
tem per a ture   va ri a ble   op er a tive
val u a ble   hŏs pit a ble   prof it a ble
ven er a ble   for mid a ble   tol er a ble
vul ner a ble   ăn swer a ble   cop u la tive

The following have the half accent on the third
syllable.

Àg ri cul ture   tab er na cle   ärch i tec ture
an ti qua ry   tran sit o ry   ar bi tra ry
ap o plex y   àu dit o ry   par si mo ny

———◦✳◦———

TABLE XXIV.

Words of four syllables; the full accent on the
second, and half accent on the fourth.

NOTE.   The terminations *ty, ry,* and *ly,* have very little accent.

Ad vi sa ble   im me di ate   vic to ri ous
ac cu mu late   im pe ri ous   vo lu min ous
ap pro pri ate   im pla ca ble   ux o ri ous
an ni hi late   in tu i tive   as păr a gus
a me na ble   la bo ri ous   ac cel er ate
ab bre vi ate   me lo di ous   ad mis si ble
al le vi ate   mys te ri ous   ad ven tur ous
cen so ri ous   no to ri ous   a dul ter ate
com mo di ous   ob se qui ous   ac cept a ble
com mu ni cate   op pro bri ous ag gran dize ment
con cu pis cence   pe nu ri ous   dis fran chise ment
com pa ra ble   pre ca ri ous   am big u ous
de plo ra ble   sa lu bri ous   am phib i ous
dis pu ta ble   spon ta ne ous a nal y sis
er ro ne ous   ter ra que ous ar tic u late
har mo ni ous   vi ca ri ous   as sas sin ate

be at i tude
ca lum ni ate
ca pit u late
cer tif i cate
ca tas tro phe
co ag u late
com bus ti ble
com mem o rate
com mis er ate
com par a tive
com pat i ble
com pend i ous
con grat u late
con spic u ous
con tem pla tive
con tempt i ble
con tig u ous
de fin i tive
de lib er ate
de riv a tive
di min u tive
e phem e ris
e piph a ny
fa cil it ate
fa nat i cism
il lus tri ous

im pet u ous
in dus tri ous
in gen u ous
in quis i tive
in vid i ous
in vin ci ble
in vis i ble
per fid i ous
per spic u ous
pre dic a ment
per plex i ty
pro mis cu ous
pa rish ion er
re cep ta cle
ri dic u lous
si mil i tude
sus cep ti ble
tem pest u ous
tu mult u ous
vi cis si tude
vo cif er ous
vo lup tu ous
u nan im ous
de bauch e ry
con form i ty
de form i ty

e nor mi ty
sub or din ate
a bom in ate
ac com mo date
a non y mous
a poc a lypse
a poc ry pha
a pos tro phe
cor rob o rate
de nom in ate
de mon stra ble
de pop u late
dis con so late
pre pos ter ous
pre rog a tive
re spons i ble
ad mis si ble
con vers a ble
re vers i ble
su per flu ous
su per la tive
pre serv a tive
ac com pa ny
dis cov er y
or
em broid er y

------◦＊◦------

TABLE XXV.

THERE are five states of human life, in-
fancy, childhood, youth, manhood, and old
age. The infant is helpless; he is nour-
ished with milk;--when he has teeth, he begins to eat bread, meat, and fruit, and is
very fond of cakes and plums. The little boy
chuses some plaything that will make a noise,
a hammer, a stick, or a whip. The little girl

loves her doll and learns to dress it. She chuses a closet for her baby-house, where she sets her doll in a little chair, by the side of a table, furnished with tea-cups as big as a thimble.

As soon as boys are large enough, they run away from home, grow fond of play, climb trees to rob birds' nests, tear their clothes, and when they come home, their parents often chastise them.—O how the rod makes their legs smart. These are naughty boys, who love play better than their books—cruel boys, who rob the birds of their eggs,—poor little birds which do no harm, which fill the air with the sweet melody of their notes, and do much good by devouring the worms, and other insects, which destroy the fruits and herbage.

Charles, how many barley corns make an inch? Three.—How many inches are in a foot? Twelve. —How many feet in a yard? Three.—How many yards in a rod, perch, or pole? Five and a half— How many rods in a mile? Three hundred and twenty.—How many rods in a furlong? Forty.— How many furlongs in a mile? Eight.—How many miles in a league? Three.—How many lines in an inch? Twelve.—What is a cubit? The length of the arm from the elbow to the end of the longest finger, which is about eighteen inches. A fathom is the distance of the ends of a man's fingers, when the arms are extended, which is about six feet.

Henry, tell me the gills in a pint. Four— Two pints make a quart, four quarts make a gallon. Barrels are of various sizes; some contain no more than twenty seven gallons, some thirty, or thirty-two, and others thirty-six. A hogshead contains sixty-three gallons; but we usually call puncheons by the name of hogsheads, and these hold about one hundred and ten gallons. A pipe contains two hogsheads, or four barrels, or about one hundred and twenty gallons.

TABLE XXVI.

Words of five syllables ; the full accent on the second.

Co tem po ra ry
de clam a to ry
de fam a to ry
dis pens a to ry
e lec tu a ry
e pis to la ry
ex clam a to ry
ex plan a to ry
ex tem po ra ry
he red it a ry
in cen di a ry
in flam ma to ry
pre lim i na ry
com mu ni ca ble
com mu ni ca tive
in vi o la ble
per spi ra to ry
de gen er a cy
con fed er a cy
con sid er a ble

pre par a to ry
pro hib it o ry
re sid u a ry
tu mult u a ry
vo cab u la ry
vo lup tu a ry
con sol a to ry
de pos it o ry
de rog a to ry
in vol un ta ry
re pos it o ry
ob serv a to ry
de lib er a tive
ef fem in a cy
in suf fer a ble
in dis so lu ble
in vul ner a ble
in vet er a cy
in ter min a ble
in tem per ate ly

———◦✳◦———

TABLE XXVII.

WILLIAM, tell me how many mills make a cent? Ten.—How many cents a dime? Ten—Tell me the other coins of the United States. Ten dimes make a dollar, ten dollars an eagle, which is a gold coin, and the largest which is coined in the United States. Dimes and dollars are silver coins. Cents are copper coins. These are new species of coin—What is the ancient manner of reckoning money? By pounds, shillings, pence, and farthings. Four farthings make a penny, twelve pence a shilling, and twenty shillings a pound.

William loves fruit. See him picking strawberries—bring him a basket—let him put the berries in a basket—and carry them to his mamma and sisters. Little boys should be kind and generous—they should always carry some fruit home for their friends. Observe the cherry-trees—see, how they begin to redden—in a few days, the cherries will be ripe; the honey-hearts, the black-hearts, and ox-hearts, how sweet they are. You must not eat too many, and make yourself sick. Fill your basket with cherries, and give them to your little friends.

Now see the pears. The harvest pear, how yellow. It is ripe, let me pick and eat it. The sugar pear, how plump and soft it is; and what a beautiful red covers one side of it. See the catherine pear, and the vergaloo, how rich, juicy, and delicious. But the peach—how it exceeds all fruit in its delicious flavor; what can equal its fragrance, and how it melts upon the tongue. The nutmeg, the rare-ripe with its blushing cheek, the white cling-stone with its crimson tints—and the lemon cling-stone with its golden hue, and all the varieties of the free-stones. Such are the rich bounties of nature, bestowed on man to please his taste, preserve his health, and draw his grateful heart towards the Author of his happiness.

REMARKS.

A wise man will consider, not so much the present pleasure and advantage of a measure, as its future consequen es.

Sudden and violent passions are seldom durable.

TABLE XXVIII.

Words of five syllables accented on the first and third.

Am bi gù i ty	reg u lar i ty
con ti gu i ty	rep re hen si ble
con tra ri e ty	rep re sen ta tive
dic ta to ri al	sat is fac to ry
ep i cu re an	sen si bil i ty
im por tu ni ty	sen su al i ty
no to ri e ty	sim i lar i ty
op por tu ni ty	sin gu lar i ty
per pe tu i ty	tes ta ment a ry
per spi cu i ty	cir cum am bi ent
pres by te ri an	com pre hen si ble
pri mo ge ni al	con san guin i ty
su per flu i ty	con tra dict o ry
tes ti mo ni al	cred i bil i ty
ac a dem ic al	di a met ric al
af fa bil i ty	el e ment a ry
al pha bet ic al	ep i dem ic al
an a lyt ic al	e van gel ic al
ar gu ment a tive	fal li bil i ty
mon o syl la ble	gen e al o gy
plau si bil i ty	hos pi tal i ty
pol y syl la ble	il le git im ate
pop u lar i ty	im per cep ti ble
pos si bil i ty	in tel lect u al
pri mo gen i ture	in tro duc to ry
prin ci pal i ty	in tre pid i ty
prob a bil i ty	ir re sist i ble
prod i gal i ty	mag na nim i ty
punc tu al i ty	met a phys ic al
pu sil lan im ous	an a tom ic al

an i mos i ty

a pos tol ic al

ar is toc ra cy

as tro nom ic al

cat e gor ic al

cu ri os i ty

di a bol ic al

et y mol o gy

gen e ros i ty

e qui pon der ant

in dis solv a ble

in ter rog a tive

met a phor ic al

pe ri od ic al

phi lo soph ic al

phys i og no my

phys i ol o gy

trig o nom e try

u ni form i ty

u ni vers i ty

em blem at ic al

ge o graph ic al

---❋---

TABLE XXIX.

LESSON I.

Be not anxious for your life, what ye shall eat, or what ye shall drink; nor for your body, what ye shall put on; for your heavenly Father knoweth that ye have need of these things.

Behold the fowls of the air: For they sow not, neither do they reap, nor gather into barns; yet your heavenly Father feedeth them.

Consider the lilies of the field, how they grow; they toil not, neither do they spin: and yet Solomon in all his glory was not arrayed like one of these.

II.

Therefore be not anxious for the good things of this life, but seek first the kingdom of heaven and its righteousness, and all these things shall be added to you.

Ask and it shall be given unto you: Seek and ye shall find: Knock and it shall be opened.

Love your enemies; bless them that curse you, do good unto them that hate you; and pray for them that scornfully use you and persecute you.

III.

When thou prayest, be not as the hypocrites, who love to pray standing in the synagogues, and in the streets, that they may be seen of men: But when thou prayest, enter into thy closet, and when thou hast shut thy door, pray to thy Father who is in secret, and thy Father who seeth in secret shall reward thee openly.

IV.

Lay not up for yourselves treasures on earth, where moth and rust doth corrupt, and where thieves break through and steal; but lay up for yourselves treasures in heaven, where neither moth nor rust doth corrupt, and where thieves do not break through and steal: For where your treasure is, there will your heart be also.

Our Saviour's Golden Rule.

ALL things which you would have men do to you, do ye the same to them; for this is the law and the prophets.

TABLE XXX.

In the following words, *tion, tian, tial,* and *tier,* are pronounced *chun, chal, chur.*

Côur tier	fus tian	com bus tion
bâs tion	mix tion	di ges tion
christ ian	ce lês tial	ad mix tion

And in all words where *t* is preceded by *s* or *x.*

In all other words *tion* is pronounced *shun;* as are also *cion, cyon, tion.* Thus, *motion, corrcion, halcyon, mansion,* are pronounced *moshun, coershun, halshun, manshun. Cial* is pronounced *shal.*

Words of two syllables accented on the first.

Mô tion	por tion	sta tion
na tion	po tion	âc tion
no tion	ra tion	dic tion

G

fac tion	men tion	ses sion
fic tion	mis sion	ten sion
frac tion	pas sion	unc tion
fric tion	pen sion	auc tion
func tion	sanc tion	op tion
man sion	sec tion	ver sion

Words of three syllables accented on the second.

Ces sa tion	com mis sion	pro tec tion
com mo tion	com pres sion	pre emp tion
de vo tion	con fes sion	re demp tion
plant a tion	con sump tion	re flec tion
pol lu tion	con ven tion	sub jec tion
pro por tion	con vic tion	suc ces sion
re la tion	cor rec tion	sus pen sion
sal va tion	de cep tion	as per sion
fi du cial	de scrip tion	as ser tion
ad mis sion	di rec tion	a ver sion
af fec tion	dis tinc tion	con ver sion
af flic tion	ex cep tion	de ser tion
as cen sion	ex pres sion	dis per sion
as sump tion	in flic tion	re ver sion
at ten tion	ob jec tion	sub ver sion
col lec tion	pro fes sion	sub stan tial

Words of four syllables ; the full accent on the third, and the half accent on the first.

Ac cept a tion	cal cu la tion
ac cu sa tion	con dem na tion
ad mi ra tion	con gre ga tion
ad o ra tion	con sti tu tion
ag gra va tion	con tem pla tion
ap pro ba tion	cul ti va tion
av o ca tion	dec la ra tion

des o la tion
ed u ca tion
el o cu tion
em u la tion
ex pect a tion
hab it a tion
in clin a tion
in sti tu tion
med it a tion
mod e ra tion
nav i ga tion
ob serv a tion
per se cu tion
pres erv a tion
proc la ma tion
pub lic a tion
ref orm a tion

res o lu tion
rev e la tion
rev o lu tion
sep a ra tion
sup pli ca tion
trib u la tion
vi o la tion
vis it a tion
ap pre hen sion
com pre hen sion
con de scen sion
con tra dic tion
ju ris dic tion
res ur rec tion
sat is fac tion
aug ment a tion
al ter a tion

Words of five syllables, accented on the first and fourth.

Am pli fi ca tion
qual i fi ca tion
ed i fi ca tion
as so ci a tion
mul ti pli ca tion
con tin u a tion
rat i fi ca tion
sanc ti fi ca tion
sig ni fi ca tion
cir cum lo cu tion
cir cum val la tion
com mem mo ra tion

con fed e ra tion
con grat u la tion
con so ci a tion
or gan i za tion
co op e ra tion
glo ri fi ca tion
pro nun ci a tion
pro pi ti a tion
re gen e ra tion
re nun ci a tion
re tal i a tion
ar gu ment a tion

Note. *As-sas-sin-a-tion, de-nom-i-na-tion, de-ter-min-a-tion, il-lu-min-a-tion,* have the second and fourth syllables accented, and *tran-sub-stan-ti-a-tion,* has an accent on the first, third, and fifth syllables. *Con-sub-stan-ti-a-tion,* follows the same rule.

TABLE XXXI.

Familiar Lessons.

HENRY is a good boy. Come here, Henry, let me hear you read. Can you spell easy words? Hold up your head; speak loud and plain. Keep your book clean: do not tear it.

John, keep your seat; and sit still. You must not say a word, nor laugh, nor play. Look on your book, learn your letters, study your lesson.

Charles, can you count? Try. One, two, three, four, five, six, seven, eight, nine, ten.—Well said; now spell bird. B-i-r-d. How the birds sing and hop from branch to branch among the trees. They make nests too, and lay eggs; then sit on their eggs, and hatch young birds. Dear little birds, how they sing and play. You must not rob their nests, nor kill their young: it is cruel.

Moses, see the cat, how quiet she lies by the fire. Puss catches mice. Did you ever see puss watching for mice? How still and sly! She creeps along, fixing her eyes steady on the place where the mouse lies. As soon as she gets near enough, she darts forward, and seizes the little victim by the neck. Now the little mouse will do no more mischief.

See the little helpless kittens. How warm and quiet they lie in their bed, while puss is gone. Take them in your hands, don't hurt them; they are harmless, and do no hurt. They will not bite nor scratch. Lay them down softly, and let them go to sleep.

George, the sun has risen, and it is time for you to rise. See the sun, how it shines: it dispels the darkness of night, and makes all nature gay and cheerful. Get up, Charles; wash your hands, comb your hair, and get ready for breakfast. What are we to have for breakfast? Bread and milk.

This is the best food for little boys. Sometimes we have coffee or tea, and toast. Sometimes we have cakes.

James, hold your spoon in your right hand; and if you use a knife and fork, hold the knife in your right hand. Do not eat fast; hungry boys are apt to eat fast, like the pigs. Never waste your bread; bread is gained by the sweat of the brow. Your father plants or sows corn; corn grows in the field; when it is ripe, it is cut, and put in the barn; then it is threshed out of the ears, and sent to a mill. the mill grinds it. and the bolter separates the bran from the flour. Flour is wet with water or milk; and with a little yeast or leaven, it is raised, and made light; this is called dough: dough is baked in an oven, or pan, and makes bread.

THE SISTERS.

Emily, look at the flowers in the garden. What a charming sight. How the tulips adorn the borders of the alleys, dressing them with gayety. Soon the sweet pinks will deck the beds; and the fragrant roses perfume the air. Take care of the sweet-williams, the jonquils, and the artemisia. See the honey-suckle, how it winds about the column, and climbs along the margin of the windows. Now it is in bloom, how fragrant the air around it; how sweet the perfume, after a gentle shower, or amidst the soft dews of the evening. Such are the charms of youth, when robed in innocence; such is the bloom of life, when decked with modesty, and a sweet temper—— Come, my child, let me hear your song.

The Rose.

The rose had been wash'd, lately wash'd in a show'r,
   That Julia to Emma convey'd;
A plentiful moisture encumber'd the flow'r,
   And weigh'd down its beautiful head.

The cup was all fill'd, and the leaves were all wet,
   And seem'd, at a fanciful view,
To weep with regret, for the buds it had left
   On the flourishing bush where it grew.

I hastily seiz'd it, unfit as it was
   For a nosegay, so dripping and drown'd;
And shaking it rudely—too rudely, alas!
   I snapt it—it fell to the ground.

"And such," I exclaim'd, "is the pitiless part
   " Some act by the delicate mind;
" Regardless of wronging and breaking a heart
   " Already to sorrow resign'd.

" This beautiful rose, had I shaken it less,
   " Might have bloom'd with the owner a while;
" And the tear that is wip'd, with a little address,
   " May be follow'd, perhaps, with a smile."

Julia, rise in the morning betimes, dress the borders of the flower beds, pull up the noxious weeds, water the thirsty roots. See how the plants wither for want of rain. The flowers fade, the leaves shrivel and droop. Bring a little water to refresh them. Now the plants look green and fresh; the weeds which shaded or robbed their roots of moisture, are removed, and the plants will thrive. Does the heart want culture? Weed out the noxious passions from the heart, as you would hurtful plants from among the flowers. Cherish the virtues—love, kindness, meekness, modesty, goodness. Let them thrive, and produce their natural fruit, pure happiness, and joys serene through life.

Look to the gentle lambs, how innocent and playful; how agreeable to the sight; how pleasant the task to feed them; how grateful they are for your care. Julia, let me hear your song.

The Lamb.

A young feeble Lamb, as Emily pass'd,
   In pity she turn'd to behold:
How it shiver'd and shrunk from the merciless blast,
   Then fell all benumb'd with the cold.

She rais'd it, and touch'd with the innocent's fate,
  Its soft form to her bosom she prest ;
But the tender relief was afforded too late,
  It bleated, and died on her breast.

The moralist then, as the corse she resign'd,
  And weeping, spring-flowers o'er it laid,
Thus mus'd, " So it fares with the delicate mind,
  " To the tempest of fortune betray'd :

" Too tender, like thee, the rude shock to sustain,
  " And deni'd the relief which would save,
" She's lost, and when pity and kindness are vain,
  " Thus we dress the poor sufferer's grave."

Harriet, bring your book, let me hear you read.
What book have you ? Let me see : a little volume
of poems. How many can you repeat ? Let me
hear my dear Harriet speak one.

The Bird's Nest.

Yes, little nest, I'll hold you fast,
  And little birds, one, two, three, four ;
I've watch'd you long, you're mine at last ;
  Poor little things, you'll 'scape no more.

Chirp, cry, and flutter, as you will,
  Ah ! simple rebels, 'tis in vain ;
Your little wings are unfledg'd still,
  How can you freedom then obtain ?

What note of sorrow strikes my ear ;
  Is it their mother thus distrest ?
Ah yes, and see, their father dear
  Flies round and round, to seek their nest.

And is it I who cause their moan ?
  I, who so oft in summer's heat,
Beneath yon oak have laid me down
  To listen to their songs so sweet ?

If from my tender mother's side,
  Some wicked wretch should make me fly,
Full well I know, 'twould her betide,
  To break her heart, to sink, to die.

And shall I then so cruel prove,
  Your little ones to force away !
No, no ; together live and love ;
  See here they are—take them, I pray.

Teach them in yonder wood to fly,
    And let them your sweet warbling hear,
Till their own wings can soar as high,
    And their own notes may sound as clear.

Go, gentle birds; go, free as air,
    While oft again in summer's heat,
To yonder oak I will repair,
    And listen to your song so sweet.

Mary, what a charming little sonnet your sister Harriet has repeated. Come, my sweet girl, you must let me hear what you can say. But stop, let me see your work. Your little fingers are very handy with a needle. Very pretty indeed; very pretty work. What small stitches. You shall hem and mark all your papa's handkerchiefs, and very soon you shall work a muslin frock for yourself. Now, my girl, let me hear you repeat some verses.

On a Goldfinch starved in his Cage.

Time was when I was free as air,
The thistle's downy seed my fare,
    My drink the morning dew;
I perch'd at will on every spray,
My form genteel, my plumage gay.
    My strains for ever new.

But gaudy plumage, sprightly strain,
And form genteel, were all in vain,
    And of a transient date;
For caught and cag'd, and starv'd to death,
In dying sighs, my little breath
    Soon pass'd the wiry grate.

Thanks, little Miss, for all my woes,
And thanks for this effectual close,
    And cure of every ill:
More cruelty could none express;
And I, if you had shown me less,
    Had been your pris'ner still.

Precepts concerning the social relations.

ART thou a young man, seeking for a partner for life? Obey the ordinance of God, and become a useful member of society. But be not in haste to marry, and let thy choice be directed by wisdom.

Is a woman devoted to dress and amusement? Is she delighted with her own praise, or an admirer of her own beauty? Is she given to much talking and loud laughter? If her feet abide not at home, and her eyes rove with boldness on the faces of men—turn thy feet from her, and suffer not thy heart to be ensnared by thy fancy.

But when thou findest sensibility of heart joined with softness of manners; an accomplished mind and religion, united with sweetness of temper, modest deportment, and a love of domestic life—Such is the woman who will divide the sorrows, and double the joys of thy life. Take her to thyself; she is worthy to be thy nearest friend, thy companion, the wife of thy bosom.

Art thou a young woman, wishing to know thy future destiny? Be cautious in listening to the addresses of men. Art thou pleased with smiles and flattering words? Remember that man often smiles and flatters most, when he would betray thee.

Listen to no soft persuasion, till a long acquaintance, and a steady, respectful conduct have given thee proof of the pure attachment and honorable views of thy lover. Is thy suitor addicted to low vices? is he profane? is he a gambler? a tippler? a spendthrift? a haunter of taverns? has he lived in idleness and pleasure? has he acquired a contempt for thy sex in vile company? and above all, is he a scoffer at religion?—Banish such a man from thy presence; his heart is false, and his hand would lead thee to wretchedness and ruin.

Art thou a husband? Treat thy wife with tenderness and respect; reprove her faults with gentleness; be faithful to her in love; give up thy heart to her in confidence, and alleviate her cares.

Art thou a wife? Respect thy husband; oppose him not unreasonably, but yield thy will to his, and thou shalt be blest with peace and concord; study to make him respectable, as well for thine own sake, as for his; hide his faults; be constant in thy love; and devote thy time to the care and education of the dear pledges of thy love.

Art thou a parent? Teach thy children obedience; teach them temperance, justice, diligence in useful occupations; teach them science; teach them the social virtues, and fortify thy precepts by thine own example; above all, teach them religion. Science and virtue will make them respectable in this life—religion and piety alone can secure to them happiness in the life to come.

Art thou a brother or a sister? Honor thy character by living in the bonds of affection with thy brethren. Be kind; be condescending. Is thy brother in adversity? assist him; if thy sister is in distress, administer to her necessities and alleviate her cares.

Art thou a son or a daughter? Be grateful to thy father, for he gave thee life; and to thy mother, for she sustained thee. Piety in a child is sweeter than the incense of Persia, yea, more delicious than odors, wafted, by western gales, from a field of Arabian spices. Hear the words of thy father, for they are spoken for thy good: give ear to the admonitions of thy mother, for they proceed from her tenderest love. Honor their gray hairs, and support them in the evening of life: and thine own children, in reverence of thy example, shall repay thy piety with filial love and duty.

FABLE I.

Of the Boy that stole Apples.

AN old man found a rude boy upon one of his trees stealing Apples, and desired him to come down; but the young Sauce-box told him plainly he would not. Wont you? said the old Man, then I will fetch you down; so he pulled up some tufts of Grass, and threw at him; but this only made the Youngster laugh, to think the old Man should pretend to beat him down from the tree with grass only.

Well, well, said the old Man, if neither words nor grass will do, I must try what virtue there is in Stones; so the old man pelted him heartily with stones; which soon made the young Chap hasten down from the tree and beg the old Man's pardon.

MORAL.

If good words and gentle means will not reclaim the wicked, they must be dealt with in a more severe manner.

TABLE XXXII.

In all words ending in *ow* unaccented, *w* is silent, and *o* has its first sound. Many of these words are corrupted in vulgar pronunciation; *follow* is called *foller*, &c. for which reason the words of this class are collected in the following table.

Bår row	gal lows	nar row	win dew
bel low	bel lows	hol low	win now
bil low	har row	shad ow	yel low
bur row	cal low	shal low	bôr row
el bow	mal lows	spar row	fol low
fel low	mar row	tal low	mor row
fal low	mead ow	whit low	sor row
far row	mel low	wid ow	wal low
fur row	min now	wil low	swal low

———————◦*◦———————

TABLE XXXIII.

In the following words, *si* sound like *zh*. Thus, *confu-sion* is pronounced *confu-zhun*; *bra-sier*, *bra-zhur*; *o-sier*, *o-zhur*; *vis-ion*, *rizh-un*; *pleas-ure*, *pleazh-ur*.

NOTE. In this and the following table, the figures show the accented syllables, without any other direction.

Brå sier	con fu sion	il lu sion
cro sier	con tu sion	in tru sion
gla zier	de lu sion	in fu sion
o sier	dif fu sion	pro fu sion
ra sure	ef fu sion	oc ca sion
ho sier	ex clu sion	ob tru sion
sei zure	ex plo sion	vis ion
fu sion	e va sion	meas ure
am bro sial	a bra sion	pleas ure
ad he sion	cor ro sion	treas ure
al lu sion	de tru sion	leis ure
co he sion	dis plo sion	az ure
col lu sion	in clo sure	ad scis ion
con clu sion	e ro sion	col lis ion

con cis ion   e lis ion   in cis ion
di vis ion   e lys ian   al lis ion
de cis ion   pre cis ion   re cis ion
de ris ion   pro vis ion   cir cum cis ion

The compounds and derivatives follow the same rule.

FABLE II.

The country Maid and her Milk pail.

WHEN men suffer their imaginations to amuse them with the prospect of distant and uncertain improvements of their condition, they frequently sustain real losses, by their inattention to those affairs in which they are immediately concerned.

A country Maid was walking very deliberately with a pail of milk upon her head, when she fell into the following train of reflections: The money for which I shall sell this milk, will enable me to increase my stock of eggs to three hundred. These eggs, allowing for what may prove addle, and what may be destroyed by vermin, will produce at least two hundred and fifty chickens. The chickens will be fit to carry to market about Christmas, when poultry always bears a good price; so that by May day I cannot fail of having money enough to purchase a new gown. Green—let me consider—yes, green becomes my complexion best, and green it shall be. In this dress I will go to the fair, where all the young fellows will strive to have me for a partner; but I shall perhaps refuse every one of them, and with an air of disdain toss from them. Transported with this triumphant thought, she could not forbear acting with her head what thus passed in her imagination, when down came the pail of milk, and with it all her imaginary happiness.

TABLE XXXIV.

Words in which *cie, sie,* and *tie,* are pronounced *she; tia* and *cia, sha; cious* and *tious,* shus. Thus, *ancient, partial, captious,* are pronounced, *anshent, parshal, capshus.* This rule will be sufficient to direct the learner to a right pronunciation, without distinguishing the silent letters.

Grė cian	tran sient	ex pa tiate
gra cious	lus cious	fa ce tious
pa tient	cảu tious	fal la cious
quo tient	pår tial	to ro cious
spa cious	cồn science	in gra tiate
spe cious	con scious	lo qua cious
spe cies*	ap prė ciate	ne go ciate
so cial	as so ciate	pro pa cious
sa tiate	au da cious	rœ pa cious
ån cient	ca pa cious	sa ga cious
cap tious	con so ciate	se qua cious
fac tious	dis so ciate	te na cious
fic tious	e ma ciate	vex a tious
nup tial	ex cru ciate	vi va cious

* Pronounced *speshis.*

vo ra cious	pro vin cial	cir cum stån tial
an nůn ciate	pru den tial	con sci en tious
con ten tious	sen ten tious	con se quen tial
cre den tials	sub stan tiate	con fi den tial
e nun ciate	com mer cial	pen i ten tial
es sen tial	con tu må cious†	pes ti len tial
in fec tious	ef fi ca cious	prov i den tial
li cen tiate	os ten ta tious	rev e ren tial
om nis cience	per spi ca cious	res i den tia ry
po ten tial	per ti na cious	e qui nốc tial

The compounds and derivatives follow the same rule.
† The words of four syllables have the half accent on the first.

FABLE III.

The Fox and the Swallow.

ARISTOTLE informs us, that the following fable was spoken by Esop to the Samians, on a debate upon changing their ministers, who were accused of plundering the commonwealth.

A Fox swimming across a river, happened to be entangled in some weeds that grew near the bank from which he was unable to extricate himself. As he lay thus exposed to whole swarms of flies, which were galling him and sucking his blood, a swallow, observing his distress, kindly offered to drive them away. By no means, said the Fox: for if these should be chased away, which are already sufficiently gorged, another more hungry swarm would succeed, and I should be robbed of every remaining drop of blood in my veins.

TABLE XXXV.

In the following words the vowels are short, and the accented syllable must be pronounced as though it ended with the consonant *sh.* Thus, *pre-cious, spe-cial, effi-cient, logi-cian, mili-tia, addi-tion,* are pronounced, *presh-us, spesh-ul, effish-ent, logish-an, milish-a, addish-on.* These words will serve as examples for the following table.

Pre cious	ef fi cient	per di tion
spe cial	es pe cial	per ni cious
vi cious	fla gi tious	pe ti tion
vi tiate	fru i tion	pro fi cient
ad di tion	ju di cial	phy si cian
am bi tion	lo gi cian	po si tion
aus pi cious	ma gi cian	pro pi tious
ca pri cious	ma li cious	se di tion
co mi tial	mi li tia	se di tious
con di tion	mu si cian	sol sti tial
cog ni tion	nu tri tion	suf fi cient
con tri tion	no vi ciate	sus pi cious
de fi cient	of fi ciate	trans i tion
de li cious	of fi cial	vo li tion
dis cre tion	of fi cious	ab o li tion*
dis cu tient	pa tri cian	ac qui si tion
e di tion	par ti tion	ad mo ni tion

* The words of four syllables have a half accent on the first, except *practitioner. Arithmetician* and *supposititious* have the half accent on the second, *academician* and *mathematician* on the first.

ad ven ti tious	prej u di cial	co a li tion
am mu ni tion	pol i ti cian	com pe ti tion
ap pa ri tion	prop o si tion	com po si tion
ar ti fi cial	prep o si tion	def i ni tion
ad sci ti tious	pro hi bi tion	dem o li tion
ap po si tion	rhet o ri cian	dep o si tion
eb ul li tion	su per fi cial	dis po si tion
er u di tion	su per sti tion	prac ti tion er
ex hi bi tion	sup po si tion	a rith me ti cian
ex po si tion	sur rep ti tious	ac a de mi cian
im po si tion	av a ri cious	sup pos i ti tious
op po si tion	ben e fi cial	math e ma ti cian

The compounds and derivatives follow the same rule.

———◆◆———

In the following words, the consonant *q* terminates a syllable; but perhaps the ease of the learner may render a different division more eligible.

2	li quor	an ti qui ty
E qui ty	li que fy	in i qui.ty
e qui ta ble	li qui date	in i qui tous
li quid	la quey	ob li qui ty

SELECT SENTENCES.

Never speak of a man's virtues to his face, nor of his faults behind his back; thus you will equally avoid flattery which is disgusting, and slander which is criminal.

If you are poor, labour will procure you food and clothing—if you are rich, it will strengthen the body, invigorate the mind, and keep you from vice.—Every man therefore should be busy in some employment

FABLE IV.
The Cat and the Rat.

A CERTAIN Cat had made such unmerciful havoc among the vermin of her neighborhood, that not a single Rat or Mouse dared venture to appear abroad. Puss was soon convinced, that if affairs remained in their present situation, she must be totally unsupplied with provision. After mature deliberation therefore, she resolved to have recourse to stratagem. For this purpose, she suspended herself from a hook with her head downwards, pretending to be dead. The Rats and Mice, as they peeped from their holes, observing her in this dangling attitude, concluded she was hanging for some misdemeanor; and with great joy immediately sallied forth in quest of their prey. Puss, as soon as a sufficient number were collected together, quitting her hold, dropped into the midst of them; and very few had the fortune to make good their retreat. This artifice having succeeded so well, she was encouraged to try the event of a second. Accordingly she whitened her coat all over, by rolling herself in a heap of flour. and in this disguise, lay concealed in the bottom of a meal tub. This stratagem was executed in general with the same effect as the former. But an old experienced Rat, altogether as cunning as his adversary, was not so easily ensnared. I don't much like, said he, that white heap yonder: Something whispers me there is mischief concealed under it. 'Tis true it may be meal; but it may likewise be something that I should not relish quite so well. There can be no harm at least in keeping at a proper distance; for caution, I am sure, is the parent of safety.

TABLE XXXVI.

In the following table, *i* before a vowel sounds like **y at the begin-**ning of words, as in *junior, filial, dominion,* which are pronounced *junyur, filyal, dominyon.*

Fól io	mill ion	in gen ious
jun ior	min ion	bat tál ion
sol dier*	pill ion	ci vil ian
sav ior	pin ion	com pan ion
seign ior	trill ion	con nex ion
un ion	trunn ion	de flux ion
al ien	val iant	do min ion
gen ial	cull ion	fa mil iar
gen ius	runn ion	o pin ion
anx ioust†	scull ion	pa vil ion
bdell ium	bull ion	post ill ion
bil ious	cóll ier	punc til io
bill iards	pon iard	ras cal ion
bill ions	ón ion	re bell ion
brill iant	be háv iour	se ragl io
bagn io	com mun ion	ver mil ion
fil ial	par hel ion	aux il ia ry
flex ion	pe cul iar	min ia ture
flux ion	con ven ient	pe cún ia ry

* Pronounced sol-ger.   † Pronounced ank-shus.

FABLE V.

The Fox and the Bramble.

A FOX, closely pursued by a pack of Dogs, took shelter under the covert of a Bramble. He rejoiced in this asylum; and for a while, was very happy; but soon found that if he attempted to stir, he was wounded by thorns and prickles on every side. However, making a virtue of necessity, he forbore to complain; and comforted himself with reflecting that no bliss is perfect; that good and evil are mixed, and flow from the same fountain. These Briars, indeed, said he, will tear my skin a little, yet they keep off the dogs. For the sake of the good then let me bear the evil with patience; each bitter has its sweet; and these Brambles. though they wound my flesh, preserve my life from danger.

TABLE XXXVII.

The first sound of *th*, as in *think*.

1	the o rem	ca thar tic
E ther	the a ter	en thu si asm
ja cinth	hy a cinth	an tip a thy
the sis	cath o lic	pa renth e sis
ze nith	ep i thet	a rith me tic
thun der	lab y rinth	an tith e sis
meth od	leth ar gy	mis an thro py
an them	pleth o ry	phi lan thro py
dip thong	sym pa thy	can thar i des
eth ics	am a ranth	the oc ra cy
pan ther	am e thyst	the ol o gy
sab bath	ap a thy	the od o lite
thim ble	can the rus	ther mom e ter
this tle	math e sis	au thor i ty
thurs day	syn the sis	ca thol i con
trip thong	pan the on	my thol o gy
en thral	c the re al	or thog ra phy
ath wart	can tha ris	hy poth e sis
be troth	ca the dral	li thog ra phy
thir ty	u re thra	li thot o my
thor ough	au then tic	a poth e ca ry
thir teen	pa thet ic	ap o the o sis
ou	syn thet ic	pol y the ism
thou sand	a can thus	bib li o the cal
a the ism	ath let ic	ich thy ol o gy
the o ry	me theg lin	or ni thol o gy

Second sound of *th*, as in *thou*.

ei ther	rath er	hith er	weath er
nei ther	fath om	leath er	with er
hea then	feath er	fur ther	wheth er
cloth ier	gath er	breth ren	neth er

weth er	whith er	brôth er	be queath
prith ee	fá ther	wor thy	an ôth er
bur then	far thing	moth er	to gêth er
sovth ern	far ther	smoth er	lôg a rithms
teth er	pôth er	oth er	nèv er the lèss
thith er	broth el	be nèath	

The derivatives follow the same rule.

FABLE VI.

The Bear and the two Friends.

TWO friends, setting out together upon a journey, which led through a dangerous forest, mutually promised to assist each other, if they should happen to be assaulted. They had not proceeded far, before they perceived a Bear making towards them with great rage.

There were no hopes in flight ; but one of them, being very active, sprung up into a tree ; upon which the other, throwing himself flat on the ground, held his breath and pretended to be dead ; remembering to have heard it asserted, that this creature will not prey upon a dead carcase. The bear came up, and after smelling to him some time, left him, and went on.—When he was fairly out of sight and hearing, the hero from the tree called out—Well, my friend, what said the bear? he seemed to whisper you very closely. He did so, replied the other, and gave me this good piece of advice, never to associate with a wretch, who in the hour of danger, will desert his friend.

TABLE XXXVIII.

Words in which *ch* have the sound of *k*.

Christ	chŏl ic	or ches ter
chyle	chol er	och i my
scheme	schol ar	chi mé ra
ache	mon arch	pa ro chi al
chăsm	schir rous	cha mel ion
chrism	stŏm ach	tri băc chus
chŏrd	pà tri arch	chro mat ic
loch	eu cha rist	me chan ic
schŏol	ån ar chy	ca chex y
oi	chrys o lite	cha lib e ate
choir	char ac ter	a nach ro nism
chŏ rus	cat e chism	syn ec do che
te trarch	pen ta teuch	pyr rhich i us
cha os	sep ul cher	am phib ri chus
cho ral	tech nic al	měl an cho ly
e poch	al chy my	chro nŏl o gy
o cher	an cho ret	chi rog ra phy
tro chee	brach i al	cho rog ra phy
ån chor	lach ry mal	chro nom e ter
christ en	mach in ate	the om a chy
chem ist	sac char ine	an ti băc chus
ech o	syn chro nism	căt e chĕt ic al
chal ice	mich ael mas	bac chan ăl ian
sched ule	chŏr is ter	cat e chu men
pas chal	chron i cle	ich thy ŏl o gy

FABLE VII.

The two Dogs.

HASTY and inconsiderate connexions are generally attended with great disadvantages; and much of every man's good or ill fortune, depends upon the choice he makes of his friends.

A good-natured Spaniel overtook a surly Mastiff, as he was travelling upon the high road. Tray, although an entire stranger to Tiger, very civilly accosted him; and if it would be no interruption, he said, he should be glad to bear him company on his way. Tiger, who happened not to be altogether in so growling a mood as usual, accepted the proposal; and they very amicably pursued their journey together. In the midst of their conversation, they arrived at the next village, where Tiger began to display his malignant disposition, by an unprovoked attack upon every dog he met. The villagers immediately sallied forth with great indignation, to rescue their respective favorites; and falling upon our two friends, without distinction or mercy, poor Tray was most cruelly treated, for no other reason, but his being found in bad company.

TABLE XXXIX.

Words of French original, in which *ch* sound like *sh*, and *i* accented, like *e* long.

Châise	fa tigue	mag a zine
châm ois*	in trigue	bomb a sin
chan cre	ma rine	man da rin
cham âde	der nier	brig a dier
cham paign	po lice	bom bard ier
fra cheur	ma chine ry	buc can ier
chi cane	chèv er il	can non ier
10	chev is ance	cap a pie
pique	chiv al ry	car bin ier
shire	deb au chée	cav a lier
10	10	cor de lier
ma chine	chev a lier	gren a dier
cash ier	chan de lier	fi nan cier
an tique	cap u chin	

* Pronounced shammy.

SELECT SENTENCES.

We may as well expect that God will make us rich without industry, as that he will make us good and happy, without our own endeavors

Zeno, hearing a young man very loquacious, told him, that men have two ears and but one tongue; therefore they should hear much and speak little.

A man who, in company, engrosses the whole conversation, always gives offence; for the company consider him as assuming a degree of superiority, and treating them all as his pupils.

The basis of all excellence in writing and conversation, is truth—truth is intellectual gold, which is as durable as it is splendid and valuable.

Faction seldom leaves a man honest, however it may find him.

FABLE VIII.

The Partial Judge.

A FARMER came to a neighboring Lawyer, expressing great concern for an accident
which he said had just happened. One of
your Oxen, continued he, has been gored by
an unlucky Bull of mine, and I should be glad
to know how I am to make you reparation.
Thou art a very honest fellow, replied the
Lawyer, and wilt not think it unreasonable
that I expect one of thy oxen in return. It is
no more than justice, quoth the Farmer, to be
sure; but what did I say?—I mistake—It is
your Bull that has killed one of *my* Oxen.
Indeed! says the Lawyer, that alters the case:
I must inquire into the affair; and if—And *if !*
said the Farmer—the business I find would
have been concluded without an *if,* had you
been as ready to do justice to others, as to exact it from them

TABLE XL.

Words in which *g* is hard before *e, i,* and *y.*

Gear	dag ger	leg ged	gherk in
geese	crag gy	pig gin	au ger
geld	bug gy	quag gy	bog gy
get	crag ged	rag ged	fog gy
gift	dig ger	rig ger	clog gy
give	dreg gy	rig gish	cog ger
gig	drug get	rug ged	dog ged
gild	drug gist	scrag ged	dog ger
gill	flag gy	scrag gy	dog gish
gimp	gib ber	shag gy	jog ger
gird	gib bous	slug gish	nog gen
girt	gid dy	snag ged	par get
girl	gig gle	sprig gy	tar get
ea ger	gig let	stag ger	gir dle
mea ger	giz zard	swag ger	be gin
gew gaw	gim blet	swag gy	wag ge ry
ti ger	hag gish	trig ger	log ger head
to ged	jag gy	twig gin	or gil lous
big gin	jag ged	twig gy	to geth er
brag ger	knag gy	wag gish	pet ti fog ger

The following are pronounced as though they were written with double *g.* Thus, finger is pronounced *fing-ger.*

Fin ger	lin ger	young er	long est
an ger	lin go	young est	strong er
hun ger	lin guist	long er	mong er

These, with their compounds and derivatives, are most of the words in the language, in which *g* has its hard sound before *e, i,* and *y.* But to these must be added the derivatives of verbs ending in *g.* Thus from *dig,* come *diggeth, diggest, digged, digging,* &c. in which *g* is hard before *e* and *i.*

TABLE XLI.

*The Boy that went to the Wood to look for Birds'
Nests, when he should have gone to School.*

WHEN Jack got up, and put on his clothes,
he thought if he could get to the wood he should
be quite well; for he thought more of a bird's
nest, than his book, that would make him wise and
great.   When he came there, he could find no
nest, but one that was on the top of a tree, and
with much ado he got up to it, and robbed it of the
eggs.—Then he tried to get down; but a branch
of the tree found a hole in the skirt of his coat, and
held him fast.   At this time he would have been
glad to be at school; for the bird in a rage at the
loss of her eggs, flew at him, and was like to pick
out his eyes.   Now it was that the sight of a man
at the foot of the tree, gave him more joy than all the
nests in the world.   This man was so kind as to
chase away the bird, and help him down from the
tree; and from that time forth he would not loiter
from school; but grew a good boy and a wise young
man; and had the praise and good will of all that
knew him.

OBSERVATIONS.

The cheerful man hears the lark in the morning; the
pensive man hears the nightingale in the evening.

He who desires no virtue in a companion, has no virtue
himself; and that state is hastening to ruin, in which no
difference is made between good and bad men.

Some men read for the purpose of learning to write;
others, for the purpose of learning to talk—the former
study for the sake of science; the latter, for the sake of
amusement.

TABLE XLII.

It is a rule in the language, that *c* and *g* are hard at the end of words, and they commonly are so at the end of syllables; but in the following table they are soft, like *s* and *j* at the end of the accented syllable. Thus, *magic, acid,* are pronounced *majic, asid,* and ought to be divided mag-ic, ac-id. It is a matter disputed by teachers which is the most eligible division—*mag-ic, ac-id,* or *ma-gic, a-cid.* However, as children acquire a habit of pronouncing *c* and *g* hard at the end of syllables, I choose not to break the practice, but have joined these consonants to the last syllable. The figures show that the vowels of the accented syllables are all short.

Má gic	pa ci fy	ex pli cit
tra gic	pa geant ry	so li cit
a gile	pa gin al	im a gine
a cid	re gi cide	re li gion
di git	re gim en	li ti gious
vi gil	re gim ent	pro di gious
fa cile	re gis ter	au da ci ty
tra gile	spe ci fy	ca pa ci ty
fri gid	spe ci men	fu ga ci ty
ri gid	ma cer ate	lo qua ci ty
pla cid	ma cil ent	men da ci ty
pi geon	ma gis trate	men di ci ty
si gil	ne ces sa ry	di la cer ate
ta cit	tra ge dy	du pli ci ty
a git ate	vi cin age	fe li ci ty
ag ger ate*	ve get ate	mu ni ci pal
le gi ble	ve get ant	an ti ci pate
fla gel et	lô gic	par ti ci pate
pre ce dent	pro cess	sim pli ci ty
pre ci pice	co git ate	me di cin al
re ci pe	pro ge ny	so li ci tude
de cim al	il li cit	per ni ci ty
de cim ate	ím pli cit	tri pli ci ty
la cer ate	e li cit	ver ti ci ty

* *g* soft.

au da ci ty	om ni gin ous	per spi ca ci ty
ex ag ger ate	ver ti gin ous	per ti na ci ty
mor da ci ty	re fri ger ate	a tro ci ty
nu ga ci ty	le gis la tion	fe ro ci ty
o pa ci ty	re cit a tion	ve lo ci ty
ra pa ci ty	sa cri le gious	rhi no ce ros
sa ga ci ty	o le a gin ous	an a lo gic al
se qua ci ty	au then ti ci ty	as tro lo gic al
vi va ci ty	e las ti ci ty	ge o lo gic al
te na ci ty	e lec tri ci ty	ped a go gic al
ve ra ci ty	du o de ci mo	phi lo lo gic al
a da gi o	ab o ri gin al	tau to lo gic al
bel li ger ent	ec cen tri ci ty	the o lo gic al
or i gin al	mu cil a gin ous	re ci pro ci ty
ar mi ger ous	mul ti pli ci ty	le ger de main

The compounds and derivatives follow the same rule.

TABLE XLIII.

Words in which *h* is pronounced before *w*, though written after it. Thus, *what, when, whisper*, are pronounced *hwat, hwen, hwisper*; that is, *hooat, hooen, hooisper.*

Whale	whelm	whit	wher ry
wheal	when	whiz	wheth er
wheat	whence	whurr	whif fle
wheel	whet	wharf	whim sey
wheeze	which	what	whin ny
while	whiff	whirl	whis per
whilst	whig	where	whis tle
whine	whim	whey	whith er
white	whin	whee dle	whit low
why	whip	whi ting	whit ster
whelk	whisk	whi tish	whit tle
whelp	whist	wher ret	whim per

The compounds and derivatives follow the same rule.

In the following, with their compounds and derivatives, *w* is silent. Whore whole who whom whoop whose

TABLE XLIV.

In the following, with their compounds and derivatives, *x* is pronounced like *gs*; *exact* is pronounced *egsact*, &c.

Ex àct	ex em pli fy	ex or bit ant
ex ist	ex an i mate	ex or di um
ex empt	ex as pe rate	ex ált
ex ult	ex ùde	ex ot ic
ex am ine	ex a men	ex on er ate
ex am ple	ex u ber ance	ex èrt
ex em plar	ex hàust	ex er cent
ex ec u tor	ex hort	èx ile

In most or all other words, *x* is pronounced like *ks*, except at the beginning of **Greek** names, where it sounds like *s*.

TABLE XLV.

The history of the Creation of the World.

IN six days God made the world, and all things that are in it. He made the Sun to shine by day, and the Moon to give light by night.—He made all the beasts that walk on the earth, all the birds that fly in the air, and all the fish that swim in the sea. Each herb, and plant, and tree, is the work of his hands. All things, both great and small, that live and move, and breathe in this wide world, to him do owe their birth, to him their life. And God saw that all the things he had made were good. But as yet there was not a man to till the ground : so God made man of the dust of the earth, and breathed into him the breath of life, and gave him rule over all that he had made. And the man gave names to all the beasts of the field, the fowls of the air, and the fish of the sea. But there was not found a help meet for man ; so God brought on him a deep sleep, and then took from his side a rib, of which he made a wife.

and gave her to the man, and her name was Eve—
And from these two came all the sons of men.

All things are known to God; though his throne of
state is far on high, yet doth his eye look down upon
us in this lower world, and see all the ways of the
sons of men.

If we go out, he marks our steps: and when we
go in, no door can shut him from us. While we are
by ourselves, he knows all our vain thoughts, and the
ends we aim at: And when we talk to friend or foe,
he hears our words, and views the good or harm we
do to them, or to ourselves.

When we pray, he notes our zeal. All the day
long he minds how we spend our time, and no dark
night can hide our works from him. If we play the
cheat, he marks the fraud, and hears the least word
of a false tongue.

He sees if our hearts are hard to the poor, or if by
alms we help their wants: If in our breast we pine
at the rich, or if we are well pleased with our own
state. He knows all that we do; and be we where
we will, he is sure to be with us.

------ ◦✳◦ ------

TABLE XLVI.

Examples of the formation of derivatives and compound words.

EXAMPLE I.

Words in which *or* or *er* are added to denote an agent.

Prim.	Deriv.	Prim.	Deriv.
Act,	act-or	in-struct,	in-struct-or
lead,	lead-er	blas-pheme,	blas-phe-mer
deal,	deal-er	cor-rect,	cor-rect-or
gain,	gain-er	dis-pose,	dis-po-ser
hate,	ha-ter	op-press.	op-press-or
cool,	cool-er	re-deem,	re-deem-er
help.	help-er	dis-sent,	dis-sent-er

EXAMPLE II.

Words to express females, or the feminine gender, formed from those which express males, or the masculine gender.

act-or,	act-ress	peer,	peer-ess
bar-on,	bar-on-ess	priest,	priest-ess
tu-tor,	tu-tor-ess	prince,	prin-cess
trait-or,	trait-ress	po-et,	po-et-ess
count,	count-ess	song-ster,	song-stress
dea-con,	dea-con-ess	li-on,	li-on-ess
duke,	duch-ess	mas-ter,	mis-tress
heir,	heir-ess	em-pe-ror,	em-press
proph-et,	proph-et-ess	test-a-tor,	test-a-trix
sor-cer-er,	sor-cer-ess	seam-ster,	seam-stress

a-dul-ter-er,	a-dul-ter-ess
em-bas-sa-dor,	em-bas-sa-dress
shep-herd,	shep-herd-ess
ben-e-fac-tor,	ben-e-fac-tress
gov-ern-or,	gov-ern-ess
mar-quis,	mar-chi-o-ness
pro-tect-or,	pro-tect-ress
ex-ec-u-tor,	ex-ec-u-trix
ad-min-is-tra-tor,	ad-min-is-tra-trix

EXAMPLE III.

Words formed by *ly* (which is a contraction of *like*) used to denote a quality, or show the manner of action, or degree of quality.

bad,	bad-ly	ab-struse,	ab-struse-ly
brave,	brave-ly	cow-ard,	cow-ard-ly
chief,	chief-ly	crook-ed,	crook-ed-ly
dark,	dark-ly	ex-act,	ex-act-ly
good,	good-ly	ef-fect-u-al,	ef-fect-u-al-ly
high,	high-ly	ex-cess-ive,	ex-cess-ive-ly
weak,	weak-ly	fa-ther,	fa-ther-ly
year,	year-ly	gal-lant,	gal-lant-ly
new,	new ly	se-date,	se-date-ly

EXAMPLE IV.

Words formed by *ful*, denoting abundance.

mer-cy,	mer-ci-ful	de-ceit,	de-ceit-ful
mourn,	mourn-ful	re-spect,	re-spect-ful
hope,	hope-ful	dis-grace,	dis-grace-ful
wish,	wish-ful	de-light,	de-light-ful
youth,	youth-ful	re-venge,	re-venge-ful
awe,	aw-ful	dis-trust,	dis-trust-ful
care,	care-ful	du-ty,	du-ti-ful

EXAMPLE V.

Words formed by *able* or *ible*, denoting power or ability.

com-mend,	com-mend-a-ble	cure,	cu-ra-ble
as-sail,	as-sail-a-ble	pay,	pay-a-ble
re-spire,	re-spi-ra-ble	sale,	sale-a-ble
per-spire,	per-spi-ra-ble	vend,	vend-i-ble
ad-vise,	ad-vi-sa-ble	test,	test-a-ble
re-verse,	re-vers-i-ble	taste,	tast-a-ble
man-age,	man-age-a-ble	tax,	tax-a-ble
cred-it,	cred-it-a-ble	tame,	tame-a-ble
prof-it,	prof-it-a-ble	rate,	ra-ta-ble

EXAMPLE VI.

Words formed by *ness*, denoting a state or condition.

good,	good-ness	shrewd,	shrewd-ness
great,	great-ness	plain,	plain-ness
rash,	rash-ness	sound,	sound-ness
bald,	bald-ness	rough,	rough-ness
hoarse,	hoarse-ness	self-ish,	self-ish-ness
blood-y,	blood-i-ness	come-ly,	come-li-ness

mis-er-a-ble,	mis-er-a-ble-ness
for-mi-da-ble,	for-mi-da-ble-ness
gra-cious,	gra-cious-ness
fa-vor-a-ble,	fa-vor-a-ble-ness
of-fen-sive,	of-fen-sive-ness

Example VII.

Words formed by *ish*, denoting quality, or a small degree of it.

ape,	a-pish	white,	whi-tish
wasp,	wasp-ish	blue,	blu-ish
wag,	wag-gish	black,	black-ish
block,	block-ish	pur-ple,	pur-plish
sour,	sour-ish	gray,	gray-ish
sweet,	sweet-ish	clown,	clown-ish

Example VIII.

Words formed by *less*, denoting destitution or absence.

art,	art-less	num-ber,	num-ber-less
grace,	grace-less	mo-tion,	mo-tion-less
shape,	shape-less	meas-ure,	meas-ure-less
need,	need-less	fa-ther,	fa-ther-less
heed,	heed-less	mo-ther,	moth-er-less
care,	care-less	pray-er,	pray-er-less

Example IX.

Words formed by *al*, denoting quality, and by *some*, denoting fulness

frac-tion,	frac-tion-al	glad,	glad-some
doc-trine,	doc-trin-al	loath,	loath-some
crime,	crim-in-al	frol-ick,	frol-ick-some
na-tion,	na-tion-al	de-light,	de-light-some

Example X.

Words formed by *ous*, and *ive*, denoting quality.

grace,	gra-cious	sport,	sport-ive
glo-ry,	glo-ri-ous	ex-pense,	ex-pens-ive
hu-mor,	hu-mor-ous	con-clude,	con-clu-sive
mel-o-dy,	me-lo-di-ous	ex-cess,	ex-cess-ive
har-mo-ny,	har-mo-ni-ous	e-lect,	e-lect-ive
vic-tor,	vic-to-ri-ous	de-cide,	de-ci-sive

Example XI.

Words formed by *age, ment, ence,* and *ance,* denoting state, condition, or action performed, &c.

pa-rent,	pa-rent-age	per-form,	per-form-ance
pat-ron,	pat-ron-age	ful-fil,	ful-fil-ment
per-son,	per-son-age	at-tain,	at-tain-ment
car-ry,	car-riage	de-pend,	de-pend-ence
mar-ry,	mar-riage	oc-cur,	oc-cur-rence
re-mit,	re-mit-tance	re-pent,	re-pent-ance

ac-com-plish,   ac-com-plish-ment
com-mand,   com-mand-ment

Example XII.

Words ending in *or* or *er,* and *ee,* the former noting the agent, and the latter the person, to whom an act is done.

les-sor',	les-see'	ap-pel-lor',	ap-pel-lee
do-nor',	do-nee'	cog-ni-zor',	cog-ni-zee
bail-or',	bail-ee'	in-dors'-er,	in-dors-ee'
as-sign-or',	as-sign-ee'	ob-li-gor',	ob-li-gee'
pay'-or,	pay-ee'	mort'-ga-ger,	mort-ga-gee'

Example XIII.

Words ending in *ity,* denoting power, capacity, state, &c.

in-firm,	in-firm-i-ty	le-gal,	le-gal-i-ty
a-ble,	a-bil-i-ty	mor-tal,	mor-tal-i-ty

pos-si-ble,   pos-si-bil-i-ty
con-form,   con-form-i-ty
chris-tian,   chris-tian-i ty
pop-u-lar,   pop-u-lar-i ty
sin-gu-lar,   sin-gu-lar-i-ty
fea-si-ble,   fea-si-bil i-ty
com-pat-i-ble,   com-pat-i-bil-i-ty
im-pen-e-tra-ble,   im-pen-e-tra-bil-i-ty

Example XIV.

Verbs or affirmations, formed by the terminations *ise* and *en.*

Gen-er-al,	gen-er-al-ize	mor-al,	mor-al-ize
le-gal,	le-gal-ize	jour-nal,	jour-nal-ize
tyr-an-ny,	tyr-an-nize	can-on,	can-on-ize
meth-od,	meth-od-ize	har-mo-ny,	har-mo-nize
au-thor,	au-thor-ize	strait,	strait-en
bas-tard,	bas-tard-ize	wide,	{ wi' den, *or*
sys-tem,	sys-tem-ize		{ wid-en
civ-il,	civ-il-ize	length,	length-en

Example XV.

Words in which the sense is changed by prefixing a syllable, or syllables.

Ap-pear,	dis-ap-pear	grow,	o-ver-grow
al-low,	dis-al-low	look,	o-ver-look
o-bey,	dis-o-bey	run,	o-ver-run
o-blige,	dis-o-blige	take,	o-ver-take
es-teem,	dis-es-teem	throw,	o-ver-throw
pos-sess,	dis-pos-sess	turn,	o-ver-turn
ap-ply,	mis-ap-ply	ad-mit,	re-ad-mit
be-have,	mis-be-have	as-sume,	re-as-sume
in-form,	mis-in-form	em-bark,	re-em-bark
de-ceive,	un-de-ceive	en-force,	re-en-force
work,	un-der-work	add,	su-per-add
op-e-rate,	co-op-er-ate	a-bound,	su-per-a-bound
en-gage,	pre-en-gage	weave,	in-ter-weave
ma-ture,	pre-ma-ture	see,	fore-see
num-ber,	out-num-ber	sight,	fore-sight
run,	out-run	plant,	trans-plant
fee-ble,	en-fee-ble	com-pose,	de-com-pose
no-ble,	en-no-ble	act,	coun-ter-act

K

Example XVI.

Names formed from qualities by change of termination.

Long, length   deep, depth   dry, drouth
strong, strength   high, highth   wide, width

Examples of various derivatives from one root, or radical word.

Boun-ty, boun-te-ous, boun-te-ous-ly, boun-te-ous-ness, boun-ti-ful, boun-ti-ful-ly, boun-ti-ful-ness.

Beau-ty, beau-te-ous, beau-te-ous-ly, beau-te-ous-ness, beau-ti-ful, beau-ti-ful-ly, beau-ti-ful-ness, beau-ti-fy.

Art, art-ful, art-ful-ly, art-ful-ness, art-less, art-less-ly, art-less-ness.

Con-form, con-form-i-ty, con-form-a-ble, con-form-a-bly, con-form-ist, con-form-a-tion, con-form-a-ble-ness.

Press, press-ure, im-press, im-press-ion, im-press-ive, im-press-ive-ly, com-press, com-press-ure, com-press-ion, com-press-i-ble, com-press-i-bil-i-ty, in-com-press-i-ble, in-com-press-i-bil-i-ty, de-press, de-press-ion, sup-press, sup-press-ion.

Grief, griev-ous, griev-ous-ly, griev-ance, ag-grieve.

At-tend, at-tend-ant, at-tend-ance, at-ten-tion, at-ten-tive, at-ten-tive-ly, at-ten-tive-ness.

Fa-vor, fa-vor-ite, fa-vor-a-ble, fa-vor-a-bly, fa-vor-a-ble-ness, fa-vor-it-ism, un-fa-vor-a-ble, un-fa-vor-a-bly, un-fa-vor-a-ble-ness, dis-fa-vor.

Compound Words.

Ale house	cop per plate	gin ger bread
ap ple tree	day light	grand child
bed fel low	di ning room	New ha ven
bed cham ber	Charles town	New york
bee hive	George town	ink stand
book sell er	dress ing room	ju ry man
but ter milk	drip ping pan	land tax
can dle stick	earth quake	lap dog
chain shot	el bow chair	moon shine
cher ry tree	fer ry man	pa per mill
ches nut tree	fire arms	ti tle page
cop y book	fire shov el	Yale col lege

OBSERVATIONS.

He seldom lives frugally, who lives by chance.

Most men are more willing to indulge in easy vices, than to practice laborious virtues.

A man may mistake the love of virtue for the practice of it; and be less a good man, than the friend of goodness;

Without frugality, none can be rich; and with it, few would be poor.

Moderation and mildness, often effect what cannot be done by force. A Persian writer finely observes, that "a gentle hand leads the elephant himself by a hair."

The most necessary part of learning is, to unlearn our errors.

Small parties make up in diligence what they want in numbers.

Some talk of subjects which they do not understand: others praise virtue, who do not practice it.

No persons are more apt to ridicule or censure others, than those who are most apt to be guilty of follies and faults.

TABLE XLVII.

Irregular words, not comprised in the foregoing tables.

Written.	Pronounced.	Written.	Pronounced.
A ny	en ny	isle	ile
bat teau	bat to	isl and	ile and
beau	bo	ma ny	men ny
beaux	boze	ocean	o shun
been	bin	says	sez
bu reau	bu ro	said	sed
bu ry	ber ry	sous	soo
bu sy	biz zy	su gar	shoog ar
co lo nel	cur nel	vis count	vi count
haut boy	ho boy	wo men	wim in

Written.	Pronounced.
Ap ro pos	ap pro po
bel les let tres	bel let ter
bu si ness	biz ness
flam beau	flam bo
che vaux de frise	shev o de freeze
en ten dre	en taun der
port man teau	port man to
right eous	ri chus

The compounds and derivatives follow the same rule.

OBSERVATIONS.

Seek a virtuous man for your friend, for a vicious man can neither love long, nor be long beloved—The friendships of the wicked are conspiracies against morality and social happiness.

More persons seek to live long, though long life is not in their power, than to live well, though a good life depends on their own will

USEFUL LESSONS.

JOHN can tell how many square rods of ground make an acre. Let me near him. Three feet make a yard; five yards and a half make a rod or perch; forty square rods make a rood or one quarter of an acre, and one hundred and sixty square rods make an acre One team will plow an acre in a day—sometimes more.

In solids, forty feet of round timber, or fifty feet of hewn timber, make a ton. A cord of wood contains one hundred and twenty-eight solid feet; that is, a pile four feet high, four feet wide, and eight feet long.

In cloth measure, two inches and a fifth make a nail —four nails, one quarter of a yard—thirty-six inches or three feet make a yard—three quarters of a yard make an ell Flemish—and five quarters make an English ell.

Let us examine the weights used in our own country. How are heavy goods weighed? By avoirdupois weight —in which sixteen drams make an ounce—sixteen ounces, one pound—twenty-eight pounds, one quarter of a hundred —four quarters, or one hundred and twelve pounds, make a hundred—and twenty hundreds, one ton.

By this weight, are sold hay, sugar, coffee, and all heavy goods and metals, except gold and silver.

What is troy weight? It is that by which is estimated the quantity of gold and silver, jewelry, and the drugs sold by the druggist and apothecary In troy weight, twenty-four grains make a pennyweight—twenty pennyweights, one ounce—and twelve ounces, one pound These are the divisions used by the silversmith and jeweller. But the apothecary uses a different division, and in his weight, twenty grains make a scruple—three scruples one dram— eight drams one ounce—and twelve ounces one pound.

The dollar is one hundred cents; but the value of a pound, shilling, and penny, is different, in different States, and in England. English money is called Sterling—One dollar is four shillings and six pence sterling—in New-England and Virginia, it is six shillings—in New-York and North Carolina, it is eight shillings—in New-Jersey, Pennsylvania, Delaware, and Maryland, it is seven shillings and six pence—in South Carolina and Georgia, it is four shillings and eight pence. But these differences give great trouble, and will soon be laid aside as useless,—all money will be reckoned in dollars and cents

INHABITANTS OF THE UNITED STATES.

Census in	1790	1800	1810	1820
Vermont	85,539	154.465	217,835	235,764
New-Hampshire	141,885	183,858	214,460	244,161
Maine	96,540	151,719	228,705	298,335
Massachusetts	378,787	422,845	472,040	523,287
Rhode-Island	68,825	69,122	76,931	83,059
Connecticut	237,946	251,002	261,942	275,248
New-York	340,120	586,050	959,049	1,372,812
New-Jersey	184,139	211,149	245,562	277,575
Pennsylvania	434,373	602,545	810,091	1,049,398
Delaware	59,094	64,273	72,674	72,749
Maryland	319,728	353,968	380,546	407,350
Virginia	747,610	886,149	974,622	1,065.366
North-Carolina . . .	393,951	478,103	555,500	638,829
South-Carolina . . .	249,073	345,591	415,115	490,309
Georgia	82,548	162,686	252,433	340,989
Kentucky	73,677	220,959	406,511	564,317
Territory N. W. of Ohio . .	35,691	45,365		
	3,929,326			
Of these are Slaves . 697,696				
Indiana		5,641	24,520	147,178
Mississippi		8,850	40,352	75,448
Tennessee		105,602	261,727	422,813
		5,309,758		
Of these are Slaves . 894,452				
Ohio			230,760	581,434
Louisiana and Orleans Territory			97,401	153,407
Illinois			12,282	55,211
Michigan Territory . . .			4,762	8,896
District of Columbia . .			24,023	33,039
			7,239,903	
Of these are Slaves 1,191,364				
Alabama				127,901
Missouri				66,586
Grand Total,				9,625,734

OBSERVATIONS AND MAXIMS.

THE path of duty, is always the path of safety.

Be very cautious in believing ill of your neighbor; but more cautious in reporting it.

It requires but little discernment to discover the imperfections of others; but much humility to acknowledge our own.

Many evils incident to human life are unavoidable; but no man is vicious, except by his own choice.

Avoid vicious company, where the good are often made bad, and the bad worse. If the good ever associate with evil men, it should be for the same reason as a physician visits the sick.—not to catch the disease, but to cure it.

Some people are lost for want of good advice, but more for want of giving heed to it.

TABLE XVIII.

The most usual Names of Men, accented.

Aa' ron	Dan' iel	Hugh
A' bel	Da' vid	Ho ra' tio
A' bram	Den' nis	Hor' ace
A'bra ham		Hez e ki' ah
Ad' am	Ed' mund	
Al' bert	Ed' ward	I' saac
Al' len	Ed' win	Is' rael
Al ex an' der	Ed' gar	Ich' a bod
Al' fred	Eg' bert	
Am' brose	E le a' zar	Ja' bez
A' mos	El' dad	Ja' cob
An' drew	E' li	James
An' tho ny	E li' as	Jef' frey
Ar' chi bald	E li' zur	Job
Ar' nold	E li' sha	Jo' el
Ar' thur	E liph' a let	John
Au' stin	E' noch	Jo' nas
A' sa hel	E' phraim	Jo' seph
A' saph	E ze' ki el	Jo si' ah
A' sa	E ras' tus	Josh' u a
Ash'er	Ez' ra	Jude
	Eb e ne' zer	Jus' tus
		Jer e mi' ah
Bar' na bas	Fran' cis	Jon' a than
Ben' ja min	Fred' er ic	Ja' red
Ben' net		Jes' se
Ber' nard	Ga' briel	
Brad' ford	George	Leon' ard
	Gid' e on	Lew' is
	Gil' bert	Lu' cius
Ca' leb	Giles	Luke
Charles	God' frey	Lem' u el
Chris' to pher	Greg' o ry	Le vi
Cor ne' li us		Lu' ther
Clark	Hen' ry	
Cyp' ri an		

Mark	Pe' ter	Ste' phen
Mar' tin	Paul	Si' las
Mat' thew	Phil' ip	
Mi' chael	Phin' e as	The' o dore
Miles		The oph' i lus
Mor' gan	Ralph	Thom' as
Mo' ses	Reu' ben	Tim' o thy
Me' dad	Rich' ard	Ti' tus
	Rob' ert	
	Ro' ger	U ri' ah
Na' than	Ru' fus	
Na than' iel		Val' en tine
Ne he mi' ah		Vin' cent
Nich' o las	Sam' u el	
Nor' man	Seth	Wal' ter
	Sil ves' ter	Will' iam
	Sim' e on	
Ob a di' ah	Si' mon	Za' doc
Ol' i ver	Sol' o mon	Zech a ri' ah

---- ✳ ----

Names of Women.

Ab' i gail	Dor' cas	Grace
A' my	Dor' o thy	
Ann	De' lia	Han' nah
An' na		Har' ri et
An' nis	El' ea nor	Hel' en
A me' lia	E li' za	Hen ri et' ta
	E liz' a beth	Hes' ter
Bridg' et	Em' ma	Hul' dah
Be lin' da	Em' i ly	
	Es' ther	Is' a bel
Car' o line	Eu' nice	
Cla ris' sa	E mil' ia	Jane
Ce' li a		Je mi' ma
	Faith	Jen' net
Deb' o rah	Flo' ra	Ju' li a
Di' nah	Fran' ces	Ju li an' a

Kath' a rine	Ma ri' a	Re bec' ca
		Ruth
Love	Nan' cy	Rose
Lu' cy		
Lyd' ia	Pa' tience	Sa' rah
Lu cre' tia	Pe nel' o pe	So phi' a
Lu cin' da	Phe' be	Sal' ly
	Phil' lis	Su san' nah
Ma' bel	Pris cil' la	Su' san
Mar' ga ret	Pru' dence	Tem' per ance
Mar' tha		
Ma' ry	Ra' chel	Ur su' la

---◦*◦---

Derivatives from Names.

Am' mon,	Am' mon ite
Ca naan,	Ca' naan ite
E' phraim,	E' phraim ite
Mo' ab,	Mo' ab ite
Cal' vin,	Cal' vin ist
Lu' ther,	Lu' ther an
Is' rael,	Is' rael ite
Rome,	Ro' man
Cor' inth,	Co rinth' i an
Ath' ens,	A the' ni an
Ha' gar,	Ha' gar enes
Ga la' tia,	Ga la' tians
Sa ma' ri a,	Sa mar' i tans
Am' a lek,	Am' a lek ite
E' dom,	E' dom ite
Beth' le hem,	Beth' le hem ite
Lon' don,	Lon' don er
Par' is,	Pa ris' ian
Ben' ja min,	Ben' ja min ite
Reu' ben,	Reu' ben ite
Jew,	Jew' ish
New ton,	New to' ni an

A lex an' dri a,	A lex an' dri an
Ci" ce ro,	Ci" ce ro' ni an
Co per' nic us,	Co per' nic an
Ep i cu' rus,	Ep i cu' re an
Gal' i lee,	Gal i le' an
Ma hom' et,	Ma hom' e tan
Sad' du cee,	Sad du ce' an
Phar' i see,	Phar i sa' ic
Pla' to,	Pla' ton ic
Pla' to nism,	Pla' to nist
Chal de' a,	Chal de' an
Cy re' ne,	Cy re' ni an
Gil' e ad,	Gil' e ad ite
Her' od,	He ro' di ans
Ish' ma el,	Ish' ma el ite
Mid' i an,	Mid' i an ite
Tyre,	'Tyr' i an

TABLE XLIX.

Names of the principal Countries on the Eastern Continent, the adjective belonging to each, the name of the People, and the chief Town or City —accented.

Country.	Adjective.	People.	Chief Cities.
A' sia,	A siat' ic,	A siat' ics	
Af' ri ca,	Af' ri can,	Af' ri cans	
Aus' tri a,	Aus' tri an,	Aus' tri ans,	Vi en na
A ra' bi a,	{ Ar' a bic, { A ra' bi an,	A ra' bi ans, or A' rabs, }	Mec' ca
Al gi'ers,	Al ge ri'ne,	Al ge ri'nes,	Al gi'ers
Brit' ain,	Brit' ish,	Brit' ons, }	Lon' don
Eng' land,	Eng' lish,	Eng' lish, }	
Scot' land,	Scotch,	Scots,	Ed' in burgh
I're land,	I' rish,	{ I' rish, or { I' rish men, }	Dub' lin
Hi ber' ni a,	Hi ber' ni an,	Hi ber' ni ans, }	

Country.	Adjective.	People.	Chief Cities.
Wales,	Welch,	Welch' men	
Bo he' mi a,	Bo he' mi an.	Bo he' mi ans,	Prague
Chi' na,	{ Chi ne'se, Chi' na,	Chi ne'se,	Pe' kin
Cor' si ca,	Cor' si can,	Cor' si cans,	Bas' tia
Den' mark,	Da nish,	Danes,	Co pen ha' gen
E' gypt,	E gyp' tian,	E gyp' tians,	{ Ca'i ro, *or* Ca'i ra
Eu' rope,	Eu ro pe' an,	Eu ro pe' ans	
Flan' ders,	Flem' ish,	Flem' ings,	{ Brus' sels
Bel' gi um,	Bel' gi an,	Bel' gi ans,	
France,	French,	French,	{ Par' is
Gaul,	{ Gal' lic, *or* Gal' li can,	Gauls,	
Fran co' ni a,	Fran co' ni an,	Fran co' ni ans,	Wurts' burg
Ger' ma ny,	{ Ger' man, Ger man' ic,	Ger' mans,	Vi en' na
Ba va' ri a,	Ba va' ri an,	Ba va' ri ans,	Mu' nich
Gen' o a,	Gen o e'se,	Gen o e'se,	{ Gen' o a
Li gu' ri a,	Li gu' ri an,	Li gu' ri ans,	
Greece,	Gre' cian,	Greeks,	Ath' ens
Hol' land,	Dutch,	Dutch, *or* Hol'landers,	{ Am' ster dam Hague
Ba ta' vi a,	Ba ta' vi an,	Ba ta' vi ans,	
Hun' ga ry,	Hun ga' ri an,	Hunga'rians,	{ Pres' burg, *or* Bu' da
It' a ly,	{ I tal' ian, I tal' ic,	I tal' ians,	Rome
I'ce land,	Ice land' ic,	I'ce land ers	
In di' a,	{ In' di an, Hin' du, Hin' doo,	In' di ans, Hin' dus, Hin' doos,	{ Del' hi Cal cut' ta
In du' stan,	Gen' too,	Gen toos,	Ma drass'
Ja pan',	Jap an e'se,	Jap an e'se	
Mi lan',	Mi lan e'se,	Mi lan e'se,	Mi lan'
Mo' roc' co,	Moors,	Moors,	Fez
Na' ples,	Ne a pol' i tan,	Ne a pol' i tans,	Na' ples

Country.	Adjective.	People.	Chief Cities.
Nor' way,	Nor we' gi an,	Nor we' gi ans,	Ber' gen
Per' sia,	Per' sian,	Per' sians,	Is pa hao
Pied mont',	Pied mon te'se,	Pied mon te'se,	Tu riu'
Po' land,	Po' lish,	Po' land ers, or Poles',	War' saw
Por' tu gal,	Por' tu guese,	Por' tu guese,	Lis' bon
Prus' sia,	Prus' sian,	Prus' sians,	Ber' lin
Rus' sia,	Rus' sian,	Rus' sians,	Pe' ters burg
Si" ci ly,	Si cil' i an,	Si cil' i ans,	Pa ler' mo
Spain,	Span' ish,	Span' iards,	Ma drid'
Sar din' i a,	Sar din' i an,	Sar din' i ans,	Cag li a' ri
Swe' den,	Swe' dish,	Swedes,	Stock' holm
Swit' zer land,	Swiss,	Swiss,	Bern, or Bas' il
Sax' o ny,	Sax' on,	Sax' ons,	Dres' den
Swa' bi a,	Swa bi an,	Swa' bi ans,	Augs' burg
Tur' key,	Turk' ish,	Turks,	Con' stan ti no' ple
Tar' ta ry,	Tar' tar, Tar ta' ri an,	Tar' tars,	To bol' ski Thi' bet
Tu' nis,	Tu nis' ian,	Tu nis' ians,	Tu' nis
Tus' ca ny,	Tus' can,	Tus' cans,	Flor' ence
Si" am,	Si am e'se,	Si am e'se,	Si am'
Ton' quin,	Ton qui ne'se,	Ton qui ne se,	Tong too'
Ven' ice,	Ve ne' tian,	Ve ne' tians,	Ven' ice

❖

IN AMERICA.

A mer' i ca,	A mer' i can,	A mer' i cans

States.	Chief Towns.	People.
New Hamp' shire,	Po'rts mouth	
Maine,	Po'rt land,	
Mas sa chu' setts,	Bos' ton,	Bos to' ni ans
Ver mont',	Mont pe' lier, Ben' ning ton, Wind' sor,	Ver mont ers

States.	Chief Towns.	People.
Rhode i's land,	Prov' i dence, New' port,	Rhode i's land ers
Con nec' ti cut,	Hart' ford, New Ha' ven, New Lon' don,	
New York,	New York, Al' ba ny,	New York' ers
New Jer' sey,	Tren' ton, E liz' a beth town, Prince' ton, New' ark	
Penn syl va' ni a,	Phil a del' phi a, Lan' cas ter,	Penn syl va' ni ans
Del' a ware,	Wil' ming ton, Dover	
Ma' ry land,	Bal' ti more, An nap' o lis,	Ma' ry land ers
Vir gin' i a,	Rich' mond, Al ex an' dri a, Nor' folk,	Vir gin' i ans
North Ca ro li' na,	New' bern, Wil' ming ton, E' den ton,	Ca ro li'n i ans
South Ca ro li' na,	Charles' ton, Co lum' bia,	
Geor' gi a,	Sa van' na, Au gus' ta,	Geor' gi ans
Ken tuck' y,	Lex' ing ton,	Ken tuck' i ans
Ten nes see',	Nash' ville,	Ten nes se' ans
O hi' o,	Co lum' bus	
Lou is ian' a,	New Or' leans,	Lou is ia' ni ans
Mis sis sip' pi,	Natch' es, Mon ti cel' lo,	Mis sis sip' pi ans
Al a ba' ma,	Mo bile', Ca ha' ba, Blake' ly	
In di an' a,	Vin cen' nes, Co' ry don,	In di an' i ans
Il li nois',	Kas kas' ki a	
Mis sou' ri,	St. Lou' is	
East Flor' i da,	St. Au gus ti' ne	
West Flor i da,	Pen sa co' la	

Provinces.	Chief Towns.	People.
Mex' i co,	Mex' i co,	Mex' i cans
Chi' lí,	St. Ja' go,	Chil' i ans
Pe ru',	Li' ma,	Pe ru' vi ans
Qui' to,	Qui' to	
Par a gua'y,	Buen' os ayres	
Bra zil',	St. Sal va do're,	Bra zil' i ans

———◦✳◦———

TABLE L.

Chief Rivers on the Eastern Continent.

IN EUROPE.

Dan' ube	Loire	Scheldt*
Don', *or*	Med' way	Sev' ern
Ta na'is	Maes	Shan' non
Drave	Mo sell'*e*	Seine
Du' ro	Nie' per, *or*	Soane
Dwi' na	Bo rist' he nes	Tay
E' bro	Nie' men	Ta' gus
Elbe	Nie' ster	Thames
Eu ro' tas	O' der	Ti' ber
Ga ro'nne	Pe ne' us	Vis' tu la
Gua' del quiv ier	Po	Vol' ga
Gua di an' a	Rhone	We' ser
Hum' ber	Rhine	

* Pronounced Shelt.

———◦✳◦———

IN ASIA.

A rax' es	Ir' tis	O' by
A' va	Jen i see'	Ox' us
Cu ban'	Kur, *or*	Pe gu'
Eu phra' tes	Cy' rus	Rha
Gan' ges	Me an' der	Ti' gris
Ma' lys	Me non'	Yel' low, *or*
In' dus, *or* Sind	Me con'	Ho ang' ho

IN AFRICA.

Ba gra' da, *or*	Sen e gal'	Or' ange
Me ger' da	Ni' ger, *or*	Gau rit'z
Nile	Jol i ba'	

Oceans.

At lan' tic	Pa cif' ic	In' di an

Seas.

Bal' tic	Eu'x ine	Me o' tis, *or*
Cas' pi an	Med i ter ra'ne an	A' zoph

Bays and Gulfs.

A dri at' ic	Cal i for' ni a	Fun' dy
Baf' fins	Ches' a peak	Hud' sons
Bis' cay	Cha leu'r	Mex' i co
Both' ni a	Fin' land	Ri ga'

Lakes in Europe and Asia.

As phal' tis	Ge ne' va	Lu ga' na
Bai' kal	Gar' da	Mag gi o re
Co' mo	Is' co	O ne' ga
Con stance'	La do' ga	Wi nan'

Mountains in Europe, Africa and Asia.

Alps	Car' mel	Ju ra
Ap' pe nines	Et' na	Py re nee's
Ar' a rat	Heck' la	Si' nai
At' las	Ho' reb	Tau' rus
Ce ven nes'	I' da	Ve su' vi us
Cau' ca sus		

IN AMERICA.

An' des, *or*	Al le ga' ny	Kit ta kin' ny
Cor dil' ler as	Kaats' kill	O le roy'

Chief Rivers in America.

Am' a zon, *or*
Mar' a non
Al' ba ny
Ap a lach' y
Ap' a lach' i co' la
Ar' kan saw
Al ta ma haw'
Au dros cog' gin

Buf' fa lo

Cum' ber land
Chat ta ho chy
Clar' en don, *or*
Cape Fear
Chow an'
Con nec' ti cut
Co lum' bi a, *or*
Ta coo' chy
Chau di e're

Del' a ware

E dis' to
Elk

Flint

Hack en sac
Hou sa ton uc
Hock hock' ing
Hud' son

Il le nois'
I' ro quois, *or*
St. Law' rence

Ja ne'i ro
James, *or*
Pow hat tan'

Kan ha way
Ken tuc' ky
Ken ne bec'

Lick' ing
La moil'

Mis sis sip' pi
Mis so rie'
Musk ing' um
Mi am' i
Mo bill'
Mis sisk' o
Mer' ri mac
Moose
Ma ken' zie

Nuse
Nel' son

O ro no'ke
O hi' o
O gee' chy
On' ion

Par a gua'y, *or*
Plate
Pa to' mac
Pearl
Pas cat' a way
Pe nob' scot
Pas sa' ic

Pe dee'

Roan o'ke
Rap pa han' noc
Rar' i ton

Sa van na
San tee'
Sa lu da
Sa til la
Sus que han' na
Schu'yl kill
Sci o ta
Sau' co
Scoo' duc
St. John
St. Ma' ry
Sev' ern
Sas ka shaw' in
So rell'
Sag u nau'

Ten nes see'
Tu' gu lo
Tom big' by

Un' ji ga
U ta was'

Wa ter ee'
Wau' bosh

York
Ya zoo'

Lakes in America.

Cay u' ga	Moose head	Su pe' ri or
Can an dai' gua	Mem fre ma' gog	Tez cu' co
Cham plain	Ot se' go	Um' ba gog
E' rie	O nei' da	Win' ni pis i o' gy
George	On ta' ri o	Win' ni pic
Hu rou	On an da' go	Wa que sa no' ga
Mish i gan'	Sen' e ka	or O' ka sa no' ke

---***---

TABLE LI.

Names of Cities, Towns, Counties, Rivers, Mountains, Lakes, Islands, Bays. &c. in America.

The following have the accent on the first syllable.

A

Ab' er corn	An do ver	Av on
Ab ing don	An ge lo	Ayers ton
Ab ing ton	An ge los	
Ab se con	An tim	**B**
Ac ton	An vill	Bairds town
Ad ams	Aq ue fort	Ba kers field
Ac worth	Arm strong	Ba kers town
Al ba ny	Ar ling ton	Ball town
Al bi on	Ar row sike	Ba' ti more
Al ford	Ar u ba	Ban gor
Al lens town	Ash burn ham	Ban ba ra
All burg	Ash by	Bar nard
Al lo way	Ash field	Bar ne velt
All saints	Ash ford	Bar ne gat
Ams bu ry	Ash ton	Bar net
Al stead	Ash we lot	Barn sta ble
Am boy	As sa bet	Barn sted
Am e lius	A thol	Bar re
Ame well	At kin son	Bar rets ton
Am herst	At tle bo *rough*	Bar ring ton
Am ster dam	Av a lon	Bart let
	A ve ril	Bar ton

Bart
Bath
Bat ten kill
Bea ver
Beau fort
Beck et
Bed ford
Bed min ster
Beek man
Belch er
Bel fast
Bel grade
Bel ling ham
Ben ning ton
Ben e dict
Ben son
Ber gen
Berk ley
Berk shire
Ber lin
Ber nards town
Bern
Ber wick
Beth a ny
Beth el
Beth le hem
Bev er ly
Bil lings port
Bir ming ham
Black stone
Bla den
Bla dens burg
Blan ca
Blan co
Blan ford
Bled soe
Blen heim
Block ley

Bloom field
Bloom ing dale
Blount
Blounts ville
Blue hill
Bol in broke
Bol ton
Bom bay
Bom ba zin
Bon a ven ture
Bon a vis ta
Bon ham town
Boone ton
Boons bo rough
Bop quam
Bor den town
Bot e tourt
Bot tle hill
Bound brook
Bour bon
Bow doin
Bow doin ham
Bow ling green
Box bo rough
Box ford
Boyl ston
Boz rah
Brad ford
Bram tree
Bran don
Bran dy wine
Bran ford
Brat tle bo rough
Breck nock
Brent wood
Bre ton
Bridge town
Bridge wa ter

Bridge port
Brid port
Brim field
Bris tol
Brom ley
Brook field
Brook lyn
Broth er ton
Brough ton
Brown field
Brun ners town
Browns ville
Bruns wick
Bru tus
Buck land
Buc kles town
Bucks town
Buck town
Bull skin
Burke
Bur ling ton
Bur ton
Bush town
Bush wick
Bus tard
But ler
But ter field
But ter hill
Bux ton
Buz zards bay
By ber ry
Bye field
By ram

C

Cab ot
Ca diz
Cal ais

Cal ders burg
Cal la o
Cal vert
Cam bridge
Cam den
Camp bell
Cam po bel lo
Camp ton
Ca naan
Can dia
Can ons burg
Can so
Can ter bu ry
Can ton
Car di gan
Car ibs
Car los
Car mel
Car mel o
Car ne ro
Carns ville
Car o line
Car ter
Car ter et
Car ters ville
Car ver
Cas co
Cas tle ton
Cas tle town
Cas well
Ca to
Cav en dish
Cay mans
Ce cil
Cen ter
Cham bers burg
Chap el hill
Chance ford

Charles ton
Charles town
Charle ton
Charle lotte
Char lottes ville
Chat ham
Chelms ford
Chel sea
Chel ten ham
Chesh ire
Ches ter
Ches ter field
Ches ter town
Chick o py
Chi ches ter
Chip pe ways
Chil mark
Chitt en den
Choc taws
Chris tians burg
Chris tian sted
Chris to phers
Church town
Ci" ce ro
Clar en don
Clarks burg
Clarkes town
Clarkes ville
Clav er ack
Clin ton
Clinch
Clos ter
Cob ham
Co bles hill
Cock burne
Cock er mouth
Coey mans
Cokes bu ry

Col ches ter
Cole brook
Con cord
Con way
Coots town
Cor inth
Cor nish
Corn wall
Cort landt
Cov en try
Cow pens
Cox hall
Crab or chard
Cran ber ry
Cra ney
Crans ton
Cra ven
Craw ford
Cross wicks
Cro ton
Crown point
Croy den
Cul pep per
Cum ber land
Cum ming ton
Cus co
Cush e tunk
Cush ing
Cus sens
Cus si tah

D

Dal ton
Dan bu ry
Dan by
Dan vers
Dan ville
Dar by

Dar i en
Dar ling ton
Dart mouth
Dau phin
Da vid son
Ded ham
Deer field
Deer ing
Den nis
Den ton
Dept ford
Der by
Der ry
Der ry field
Dig by
Digh ton
Dis mal
Don ne gal
Dor ches ter
Dor lach
Dor set
Doug las
Down ings
Dra cut
Dres den
Dro more
Drum mond
Dry den
Duck creek
Duck trap
Dud ley
Dum mer
Dum miers town
Dun cans burg
Dun der burg
Dun sta ble
Dur ham
Duch ess

Dux bo rough
Dux bu ry
Dy ber ry

E

Eas ter ton
East ham
East on
East town
Ea ton
Ea ton town
E den
Edes ton
Ed gar ton
Edge comb
Edge field
Edge mont
Ef fing ham
Egg har bor
Eg mont
Eg re mont
El bert
El bert son
Elk
Elk horn
Elk ridge
Elk ton
El ling ton
El lis
El more
Em mits burg
En field
En glish town
E no
E nos burg
Ep ping
Ep som
Er rol

Er vin
Es qui maux
Es sex
Est her town
Ens tace
Ev ans ham
Eves ham
Ex e ter

F

Fa bi us
Fair fax
Fair field
Fair lee
Falk land
Fal mouth
Fals ing ton
Fan net
Fa quier
Far ming ton
Fay ette ville
Fays town
Fed er als burg
Fells point
Fer ris burg
Fin cas tle
Find ley
Fish ers field
Fish kill
Fitch burg
Flat land
Flem ing ton
Fletch er
Flints ton
Flow er town
Floyd
Flush ing
Fol low field

For est er ton
Fram ing ham
Fran ces town
Fran cis burg
Fran cois
Frank fort
Frank lin
Franks town
Fred e ri ca
Fred e rick
Fred e ricks burg
Fred e ricks town
Free hold
Free port
Free town
Fried burg
Fried land
Fried en stadt
Fry burg
Frow sack

G

Gal en
Gal lo way
Gal way
Gard ner
Gas pee
Gates
Gay head
George town
Ger man town
Ger ma ny
Ger ry
Get tys burg
Gill
Gil lo ri
Gil man town
Gil son

Glas gow
Glas ten bu ry
Glouces ter
Glov er
Glynn
Goffs town
Golds burg
Gol phing ton
Gooch land
Gor ham
Go shen
Gos port
Go tham
Graf ton
Grain ger
Gren a dines
Gran ville
Gray
Green burg
Green cas tle
Green field
Green land
Greens burg
Greens ville
Green ville
Green wich
Green wood
Gregs town
Gro ton
Gry son
Guil ford
Gur net
Guys burg

H

Hack ets town
Had dam
Had don field

Had ley
Ha gars town
Hal lam
Hal low el
Ham den
Ham burg
Ham il ton
Ham mels town
Hamp shire
Hamp sted
Hamp ton
Han cock
Han nahs town
Han ni bal
Han o ver
Har din
Hard wick
Har dy
Har dys town
Har ford
Har lem
Har mo ny
Har mar
Har pers field
Har ple
Harps well
Har ring ton
Har ris burg
Har ri son
Har rods burg
Hart ford
Hart land
Har vard
Har wich
Har win ton
Hat burg
Hat field
Hat chy

Hat te ras
Hav er ford
Ha ver hill
Hav er straw
Haw
Hawke
Haw kins
Haw ley
Hay cock
Heath
He bron
Hec tor
Hei dle berg
Hell gate
Hem lock
Hemp field
Hen ni ker
Hen ri co
Hen ry
Her ke mer
Hert ford
Hi ats town
Hick mans
High gate
High land
Hills dale
Hills burg
Hill town
Hines burg
Hing ham
Hins dale
Hi ram
Hit ton
Ho bok
Hol den
Hol der ness
Hol land
Hol lis

Hol lis ton
Hols ton
Ho mer
Hon ey goe
Hooks town
Hoo sac
Hop kin ton
Hop kins
Hope well
Horn town
Horse neck
Hors ham
Hor ton
Ho sac
Hub bard ton
Hub ber ton
Hughs burg
Hum mels town
Hum ger ford
Hun ter don
Hun ters town
Hun ting don
Hunt ing ton
Hunts burg
Hunts ville
Hur ley
Hydes park

I

Ib ber ville
In gra ham
In ver ness
Ips wich
I ras burg
Ire dell
Ir vin
Isles burg
I slip

J

Jack son
Jack sons burg
Jaf frey
Ja go
James
James town
Jay
Jef fer son
Jek yl
Jenk in town
Jer e mie
Jer i co
Jer sey
Johns bu ry
John son
John son burg
Johns town
Johns ton
Jones
Jones burg
Jop pa
Jore
Ju dith
Ju lian
Ju li et
Ju ni us

K

Kaats kill
Keene
Kel lys burn
Ken net
Ken no mic
Ken sing ton
Kent
Kep lers
Ker is son gar

Ker shaw
Kick a-muit
Kil ling ly
Kil ling ton
Kil ling worth
Kim bec
King less
Kings bu ry
Kings ton
King wood
Kit te ry
*K*nowl ton
*K*nox
*K*noul ton
*K*nox ville
Kort right

L

Lab ra dor
Lam pe ter
Lam prey
Lan cas ter
Lang don
Lanes bo ro*ugh*
Lan sing burg
Law rence
Lau rens
Lea cock
Lees burg
Leb a non
Leeds
Le hi*gh*
Lei*c*es ter
Lem ing ton
Lemps ter
Len ox
Le o gane
Leom in ster

Le on
Leon ards town
Lev er ett
Le vi
Lew is
Lew is burg
Lew is town
Lex ing ton
Ley den
Lib er ty
Lich te nau
Lick ing
Lim er ick
Lime stone
Lin co*l*n
Lin co*l*n town
Lind ley
Litch field
Lit tle burg
Lit tle ton
Liv er more
Liv er pool
Liv ing ston
Locke
Lock arts burg
Lo gan
Logs town
Lon don der ry
Lon don grove
Look out
Lou don
Loch a bar
Lou is ville
Lou is town
Loy al soc
Lud low
Lum ber ton
Lu nen burg

Lur gan
Lut ter lock
Ly man
Lyme
Lynch burg
Lynde burg
Lyn don
Lynn
Lynn field
Ly ons
Lys tra

M

Mac o keth
Mac o pin
Mad bu ry
Mad i son
Maid stone
Maine
Make field
Mal a bar
Mal den
Mar o nec
Man ca
Man chac
Man ches ter
Man heim
Man li us
Man ning ton
Man or
Man sel
Mans field
Mar ble ton
Mar ga rets ville
Mar got
Marl bo ro*ugh*
Mar low
Mar ple

Marsh field	Mil lers town	Nau ga tuc
Mar tic	Mill stone	Nave sink
Mar tin	Mill town	Naz a reth
Mar tins burg	Mil ton	Ned dick
Mar tins ville	Min gun	Need ham
Mas co my	Min goes	Nel son
Ma son	Min i sink	Nes co pec
Mas sac	Mis tic	Nesh a noc
Mas ti gon	Mo hawk	Nev er sink
Mat thews	Monk ton	New ark
May field	Mon mouth	New burg
Mead ville	Mon son	New bu ry
Meck len burg	Mon ta gue	New bu ry port
Med field	Mont mo rin	New found land
Med ford	Moore	New ing ton
Med way	Moore field	New lin
Mend ham	Moose head	New mark et
Men don	Moore land	New ton
Mer cer	More	New town
Mer cers burg	Mor gan	Nit ta ny
Mer e dith	Mor gan town	Nix on ton
Mer i meg	Mor ris town	No ble burg
Mer i on	Mor ris ville	None such
Me ro	Moul ton berg	Noot ka
Mes sers burg	Mul li cus	Nor ridge woc
Mid dle bo rough	Mun cy	Nor ri ton
Mid dle bu ry	Mur frees burg	North bo rough
Mid dle field	My ers town	North bridge
Mid dle hook		North field
Mid dle berg	**N**	North port
Mid dle burg	Nan je my	North wood
Mid dle sex	Nan ti coke	Nor ton
Mid dle ton	Nan ti mill	Nor walk
Mid dle town	Nash	Nor way
Mid way	Nash u a	Nor wich
Miff lin	Nas sau	Not ta way
Mil ford	Natch es	Not ting ham
Mil field	Na tick	Nox an

O

Oak ham
O bed
O bi on
O cri coc
O gle thorp
O hi ope
Old town
Ons low
Or ange
Or ange burg
Or range town
Or ford
Or le ans
Or ring ton
Or wel
Os na burg.
Os si py
Os ti co
O tis field
Ot ta was
Ot ter creek
Ou li out
Ov id
Ox ford

P

Pack ers field
Pac o let
Pal a tine
Palm er
Pam ti co
Pan ton
Pa ri a
Par is
Pax tang
Par sons field

Par tridge field
Pat ter son
Pau ca tuc
Paw ling
Pauls burg
Paw let
Pax ton
Peach am
Pea cock
Pearl
Peeks kill
Pel ham
Pel i can
Pem i gon
Pem broke
Pen dle ton
Pen guin
Pen ning ton
Penns burg
Penns bu ry
Pep in
Pep per el
Pep per el burg
Pe quot
Per ki o my
Per lic an
Per son
Pe ter bo rough
Pe ters burg
Pe ters ham
Pev tons burg
Phil ip
Phil ips burg
Pick ers ville
Pic o let
Pi geon
Pike land
Pi lot town

Pinck ney
Pinck ney ville
Pis to let
Pitt
Pitts burg
Pitts field
Pitts ford
Pitts town
Plain field
Plais tow
Platts burg
Plum sted
Plym outh
Plymp ton
Po land
Pom fret
Pomp ton
Pomp ey
Pop lin
Por pess
Por ter field
Port land
Ports mouth
Pot ters
Pot ters town
Putts grove
Pout ney
Pow nal
Pow nal burg
Prai ry
Pres cott
Pres ton
Pros pect
Prov ince
Prov ince town
Pru dence
Pur rys burg
Put ney

M

Q

Qua ker town
Quee chy
Queens bu ry
Queens town
Quib ble town
Quin e baug
Quin cy
Quin e paug

R

Ra by
Rad nor
Ra leigh
Ran dolph
Ran dom
Ra pha el
Raph oc
Raw don
Rah way
Ray mond
Rayn ham
Rays town
Read field
Read ing
Red ding
Read ing town
Reeds burg
Reel foot
Reams town
Reis ters town
Rens se laer
Rens se laer wick
Rhine beck
Rich field
Rich mond
Ridge field
Rid ley
Rindge

Rin gos town
Rob ert son
Rob e son
Roch es ter
Rock bridge
Rock fish
Rock ford
Rock hill
Rock ing ham
Ro' gers ville
Rom ney
Rom o pac
Rom u lus
Rose way
Ros sig nol
Rot ter dam
Rowe
Row ley
Rox burg
Rox bu ry
Roy al ton
Roy als ton
Rum ney
Ru pert
Rus sel
Ruth er ford
Ruths burg
Rye
Rye gate

S

Sa lem
Sack ville
Sad bu ry
Sau ga tuc
Sal ford
Salis bu ry
Sam burg
Samp town

Sam son
San born ton
San co ty
Sand gate
San dis field
San down
Sand wick
San dy hook
San dys ton
Sand ford
San ger field
San ta cruse
Sas sa fras
Sau con
Sau kies
Sav age
Say brook
Scar bo rough
Scars dale
Sho dack
Shen brun
Scoo duc
Schuy ler
Scip i o
Scit u ate
Scriv en
Scroon
Sea brook
Sears burg
Sedg wick
See konk
Se gum
Sen e ka
Sev ern
Se vi er
Shafts bu ry
Sham mo ny
Sham i kin

Shap leigh	Sole bu ry	Stod dard
Sha ron	So lon	Stokes
Sharks town	Som ers	Stone ham
Sharps burg	Som er set	Ston ing ton
Shaw ny	Som ers worth	Sto no
Shaw nees	Son go	Stou e nuck
Sheep scut	South bo rough	Stough ton
Shef field	South bu ry	Stow
Shel burn	South field	Straf ford
Shel by	South ing ton	Stras burg
Shen an do ah	South wark	Strat ford
Shep herds field	South wick	Strat ham
Shep herds town	Span ish town	Strat ton
Sher burn	Spar ta	Stums town
Ship pands town	Spar tan burg	Stur bridge
Ship pens burg	Spen cer	Styx
Shir ley	Spots wood	Steu ben ville
Shong um	Spring field	Stis sick
Shore ham	Spur wing	Sud bu ry
Shrews bu ry	Squam	Suf field
Shutes bu ry	Staats burg	Suf folk
Sid ney	Staf ford	Suf frage
Sims bu ry	Stam ford	Sul li van
Sing sing	Stand ish	Su mans town
Sin i ca	Stand ford	Sum ner
San pink	Stan wix	Sun a py
Skenes burg	Starks burg	Sun bu ry
Skup per nong	States burg	Sun cook
Skip ton	Staun ton	Sun der land
Sku tock	Ster ling	Sur ry
Slab town	Steu ben	Sus sex
Smith field	Ste vens	Sut ton
Smith town	Ste vens burg	Swams cot
Smith ville	Ste ven town	Swans burg
Smyr na	Ste phen town	Swan sey
Snow hill	Still wa ter	Swan ton
Snow town	Stock bridge	Swan town
So dus	Stock port	Swedes burg

Syd ney

T

Tal bot
Tam ma ny
Tam worth
Ta ney town
Ten saw
Tar bo rough
Tar ry town
Taun ton
Teach es
Tel li co
Tem ple
Tem ple ton
Tewks bu ry
Thames
Thet ford
Thom as
Thom as town
Thomp son
Thorn bu ry
Thorn ton
Thur man
Tin i cum
Tin mouth
Tis bu ry
Tiz on
Tiv er ton
Tol land
Tomp son town
Tops field
Tops ham
Tor but
Tor ring ton
Tot te ry
Tow er hill
Towns end
Trap

Trap town
Trent
Tren ton
Troy
Tru ro
Try on
Tuck er ton
Tuf ton burg
Tul ly
Tun bridge
Tur bet
Tur key
Turn er
Twig twecs
Tyngs burg
Tyr ing ham
Tyr rel

U

Uls ter
Un der hill
U ni on
U ni ty
Up ton
U ti ca
U trecht
Ux bridge

V

Vas sal burg
Veal town
Ver non
Ver shire
Vic to ry
Vin cent
Vir gil
Vol un town

W

Wades burg

Wad me law
Wads worth
Wad ham
Waits field
Wa jo mic
Wake field
Wak a maw
Wal den
Wald burg
Wales
Wal ling ford
Wall kill
Wall pack
Wal pole
Wal sing ham
Walt ham
Wand o
Want age
Wards burg
Wards bridge
Ware
Ware ham
War min ster
Warn er
War ren
War ren ton
War ring ton
War saw
War wick
Wash ing ton
Wa ter burg
Wa ter bu ry
Wa ter ford
Wa ter town
Wa ter vliet
Waw a sink
Wayne
Waynes burg

Wears	White marsh	Wins low
Weth ers field	Whit paine	Win ter ham
Wei sen berg	White plains	Win throp
Well fleet	Whites town	Win ton
Wells	Whi ting	Wo burn
Wen dell	Whit ting ham	Wol cott
Wen ham	Wick ford	Wolf burg
Went worth	Wil bra ham	Wo mel dorf
We sel	Wilks bar re	Wood bridge
West bo rough	Will iams burg	Wood bu ry
Wes ter ly	Will iams port	Wood creek
Wes tern	Will iam son	Wood ford
West field	Will iams town	Wood stock
West ford	Wil lin burg	Woods town
West ham	Wil ling ton	Wool wich
West min ster	Wil lis	Worces ter
West more	Wil lis ton	Wor thing ton
West more land	Wills burg	Wrent ham
West on	Wil man ton	Wrights burg
West port	Wil ming ton	Wrights town
West town	Wil mot	Wy an dots
Wey mouth	Wil son ville	Wyn ton
Wey bridge	Win chen don	Wythe
Whar ton	Win ches ter	**Y**
Whate ly	Wind ham	Yad kin
Wheel ing	Win hall	Yar mouth
Whee lock	Win lock	Yonk ers
Whip pa ny	Win ni pec	York
White field	Winns burg	York town

The following have the accent on the second syllable.

A	Al gon kins	An til les
A bac' co	Al kan sas	An to ni o
A bit i bis	A me lia	A pu ri ma
A ca di a	A me ni a	A quid nec
A quac nac	An co cus	Ash cut ney
A las ka	A run del	As sin i boils

M 2

As sump tion
Au re li us
Au ro ra

B

Bald ea gle
Bal div i a
Ba leze
Bark ham sted
Bar thol o mew
Bel laire
Bell grove
Bel ore
Ber bice
Ber mu da
Ber tie
Bil ler i ca
Bo quet
Bos caw en
Brook ha ven

C

Ca bar rus
Co han sie
Ca ho ki a
Ca mil lus
Cam peach y
Caer nar von
Co nan i cut
Ca rac as
Ca ran gas
Car lisle
Cas tine
Ca taw ba
Ca val lo
Cay lo mo
Cay enne
Caz no vi a
Cham blee
Char lo tia

Che buc to
Che mung
Che raws
Chi a pa
Chop tank
Chow an
Cler mont
Chic kau go
Co do rus
Co chel mus
Co col i co
Co che cho
Cock sa kie
Co hoc sink
Co han zy
Co has set
Co hose
Cole rain
Co lum bi a
Co ne sus
Con hoc ton
Co hos
Coo saw
Cor dil le ras
Corn wal lis
Coo gras
Cow e tas
Cu ma na

D

Daw fus ky
De fi ance
De troit
Din wid die
Do min go
Du anes burg
Dum fries
Dun bar ton

Du page
Du plin

E

E liz a beth
E liz a beth town
Em ma us
Eu phra ta
Es cam bia
Eu sta tia
E so pus
Ex u ma

F

Fair ha ven
Fay ette
Fitz will iam
Flat bush
Flu van na

G

Ge ne va
Ge rards town
Go naives
Gwyn nedd
Graves end
Green bush
Guild hall

H

Ha van na
Hel e na
Hen lo pen
Hi was see
Hon du ras

J

Jac mel
Je ru sa lem

K

Kas kas ki a
Kow sa ki
Key wa wa
Kil lis ti noe
Kil ken ny
King sess ing
Kin sale
Kas kas kunk

L

La com ic
La co ni a
La goon
Le noir
Long bay
Long i sland
Long lake
Long mead ow
Lo ren zo
Lo ret to
Lou i sa
Low hill
Lu cay a
Lu cia
Lu zerne
Ly com ing
Lynn ha ven
Ly san der

M

Ma chi as
Ma cun gy
Ma con nels burg
Ma de ra
Ma hack a mac
Ma ho ney
Ma hone

Ma ho ning
Ma nal lin
Man hat tan
Ma nil lon
Ma quoit
Mar cel lus
Mar gal la way
Ma tane
Ma tau zas
Ma til da
Ma tin i cus
Mat tap o ny
Me dun cook
Me her rin
Mem ram cook
Men do za
Men ol o pen
Me thu en
Mi am i
Mis sisk o
Mine head
Mo bill
Mo he gan
Mo nic con
Mo nad noc
Mon he gan
Mo noc a sy
Mon seag
Mon tauk
Mon te go
Mont gom e ry
Mont pe lier
Mont ville
Mo rant
Mor gan za
Mo shan non
Mul be gah
Musk ing um

N

Na hant
Na mask et
Nan task et
Nan tuck et
Nan tux et
Na shon
Nas keag
Na varre
Ne pon set
Ne sham o ny*
New cas tle
New Eng land
New fane
New paltz
New Roch elle
New U trecht
Ni ag a ra
Ni pis sing
North amp ton
North cas tle
North east
North um ber land

O

Oak fus ky
Oak mul gee
O co ny
O nei da
Or chil la
Os we go
Ot se go
O was co
O we go
O wy hee

P

Pal my ra

* Pronounced Shammony.

Pa munk y
Pa nu co
Pa rai ba
Pas sump sic
Pa taps co
Pa tuck et
Pa tux et
Pau tuck et
Pau tux et
Pe gun noc
Pe jep scot
Pe quon uc
Per a mus
Per cip a ny
Per nam bu co
Perth am boy
Phi lop o lis
Py an ke tunk
Py an ke shaws
Pier mont
Pin chin a
Pi o ri as
Pla cen tia
Po kon ca
Po soom suc
Port roy al
Port penn
Po to si
Pough keep sie
Pound ridge
Presque isle
Pre sums cot
Pro tect worth

Q
Quam pea gan

R
Red hook

Re ho both
Ri van na
Rock on ca ma
Ros seau
Ro siers
Row an

S
Sag har bour
Salt ash
San dus ky
Sa rec to
Sa vil la
Sa voy
Sco har rie
Scow he gan
Se kon net
Se ba go
Se bas ti cook
Se bas tian
Sem pro ni us
Se wee
Sha wan gunk*
Shaw sheen
She nan go
She tuck et
Sche nec ta dy
Skip pac
South amp ton
South hold
Stra bane
Swan na no
Swa ta ra

T
Tap pan
Ta ba go
Ta bas co
Ta con net

Ta doo sac
Ta en sa
Tar pau lin
Ta wan dy
Ta wixt wy
Ti o ga
To mis ca ning
Tor bay
To ron to
Tor tu gas
Tou lon
Tre coth ic
Trux il lo
Tunk han noc
Ty bee
Ty rone

U
U lys ses
Ur ban na

V
Ver gennes
Ver sailles
Ve nan go

W
Wa cho vi a
Wa chu set
Wal hold ing
Wap pac a mo
Wa tau ga
Wa keag
Web ham et
West chest er
West hamp ton
West In dies
West point
Wi com i co

* Pronounced Shongum.

| Wi mac o mac | Wi nee | Wis cas set |
| Win eask | Win yaw | Wy o ming |

The following have the accent on the third syllable, and most of them a secondary accent on the first.

A

Ab be ville'
Ac a pul co
Ac co mac
Ag a men tic us
Ag a mun tic
Al a bam a
Al a chu a
Al be marl
Al le mand
Al va ra do
Am a zo ni a
Am o noo suc
Am us keag
An ah uac
An as ta sia
An ti cos ti
Ap a lach i an
Ap a lach es
Ap o quen e my
Ap po mat ox
A que doch ton
Arch i pel a go
Au gus tine

B

Bas ken ridge
Bel vi dere
Bag a duce
Beth a ba ra
Bux a loons

C

Cach i may o
Cagh ne wa ga
Cal e do ni a
Can an dai gua
Can a wisk
Can i co de o
Car ib bee
Car i coo
Car i boo
Car tha ge na
Cat a ra qua
Cat a wis sa
Cat te hunk
Chab a quid ic
Char le mont
Chat a ho chy
Chat a nu ga
Cher o kee
Chet i ma chas
Chic co mog ga
Chick a hom i ny
Chick a ma ges
Chick a saw
Chil ho wee
Chil i co the
Chil lis quac
Chim bo ra zo
Chris ti an a
Clar e mont
Cin cin na tus
Con a wa go
Con a wan go
Con dus keag
Con e dog we net
Co ne maugh

Cock a la mus
Con es te o
Con es to go
Con ga ree
Coo sa hatch y
Co to pax i
Cur ri tuc
Cus co wil la
Cus se wa ga

D

Dem e ra ra
Des e a da

E

Eb en e zer
En o ree
Es ca ta ri
Es se que bo

F

Fron ti nac
Freid en huet ten

G

Gal li op o lis
Gen e see
Gen e vieve
Grad en huet ten

I

In di an a

K

Kar a tunk
Kas ki nom pa

Kay da ros so ra
Ken ne bunk
Kick a poo
Kin der hook
Kis ke man i tas
Kit ta ning
Kit ta tin ny

L

Lach a wan na
Lech a wax en
Let ter ken ny
Lit tle comp ton

M

Mach a noy
Mag da le na
Mag e gad a vie
Ma gel lan
Ma gel la ni a
Mar a cai bo
Man a han
Mar ble head
Mar cus hook
Mar ga ret ta
Ma ri et ta
Mas sa nu ten
Mau re pas
Mel a was ka
Mem fre ma gog
Mack i naw*
Mi ro goane
Mis sin abe
Mis si quash
Mo hon ton go
Ma non ga lia
Mont re al
Mor ris se na
Moy a men sing

Mus ko gee

N

Na hun keag
Nan se mond
Nau do wes sy
Nic a ra gua
Nip e gou
Niv er nois
Nock a mix on
Nol a chuc ky

O

Oc co chap po
Oc co neach y
Oc co quan
Oc to ra ro
On a lash ka
Os sa baw
Os we gach y
Ot o gam ies

P

Pak a nok
Pan a ma
Pan i mar i bo
Pas ca go la
Pas quo tank
Pas sy unk
Pat a go ni a
Pem a quid
Pen sa co la
Per qui mins
Per ki o men
Pitts syl va ni a
Pluck e min
Po ca hon tas
Po co moke
Pont char train
Por to bel lo

Por to bac co
Put a wat o mies

Q

Quem a ho ning

R

Reg o lets
Riv er head
Rock e mo ko

S

Sag a mond
Sag a naum
Sag en da go
Sal va dore
Sar a nac
Sar a to ga
Sax e go tha
Scat e cook
Seb a cook
Sem i noles
Sin e pux ent
Scan e at e tes
Soc an da ga
Spot syl va ni a
Sur i nam

T

Tal la see
Tal a poo sy
Tap pa han noc
The a kik i
Tib e rou
Tow a men sing
To ne wan to
To to wa
Tuck a hoc
Tu cu man

---

* The popular pronunciation of Mishillimackinac.

'Tul pe hock en
'Tus ca ro ra

U

U na dil la
Vi nal ha ven

W

Wah que tank
Wil li man tic
Win ne ba go
Wy a lu sing

Wy a lux ing
Wy o noke

Y

Yu ca tan
Yoh o ga ny

The following are accented on the fourth syllable.

Can a jo har ry
Can a se ra ga
Can e de ra go
Chick a ma com i co
Cob bes e con ty
Co hon go ron to
Con e go cheag
Dam e ris cot ta
Eas tan al lee
Kish a co quil las
Mish ill i mack i nac*

Mo non ga he la
Om pom pa noo suc
Pas sam a quod dy
Pem i ge was set
Quin sig a mond
Rip pa ca noe
Sag a da hoc
Sax a pa haw
Ti con de ro ga
Wa nas pe tuck et

Pronounced Mackinaw.

Islands of the West Indies.

An guil' la
An ti' gua*
Ba ha' ma
Ber mu' da
Bar ba' does
Bar bu' da
Cur a so'
Cu' ba
Dom in i' co†
Mar tin i' co‡

Por to ri' co§
Eu sta' tia
Gre na' da
Gau da lou'pe‖
Hay' ti, *or*
His pan i o' la
Ja ma'i ca
Mar i ga lant'
Miq ue lon'
Mont ser rat'

Ne' vis
To ba' go
Trin i dad'
Sant a Cruse
St. Christ' o phers
St. Lu' cia¶
St. Mar' tins
St. Thom' as
St. Vin' cent

* Pronounced Antega.   † Domineke.   ‡ Martineke.
§ Portoreko.   ‖ Gaudaloop.   ¶ Saint Luzee.

TABLE LII.

Of Numbers.

Figures.	Letters.	Names.	Numerical Adjectives.
1	I	one	first
2	II	two	second
3	III	three	third
4	IV	four	fourth
5	V	five	fifth
6	VI	six	sixth
7	VII	seven	seventh
8	VIII	eight	eighth
9	IX	nine	ninth
10	X	ten	tenth
11	XI	eleven	eleventh
12	XII	twelve	twelfth
13	XIII	thirteen	thirteenth
14	XIV	fourteen	fourteenth
15	XV	fifteen	fifteenth
16	XVI	sixteen	sixteenth
17	XVII	seventeen	seventeenth
18	XVIII	eighteen	eighteenth
19	XIX	nineteen	nineteenth
20	XX	twenty	twentieth
30	XXX	thirty	thirtieth
40	XL	forty	fortieth
50	L	fifty	fiftieth
60	LX	sixty	sixtieth
70	LXX	seventy	seventieth
80	LXXX	eighty	eightieth
90	XC	ninety	ninetieth
100	C	one hundred	one hundredth
200	CC	two hundred	two hundredth
300	CCC	three hundred	three hundredth
400	CCCC	four hundred	four hundredth
500	D	five hundred	five hundredth
600	DC	six hundred	six hundredth
700	DCC	seven hundred	seven hundredth
800	DCCC	eight hundred	eight hundredth
900	DCCCC	nine hundred	nine hundredth
1000	M	one thousand, &c.	one thousandth
1821	MDCCCXXI	one thousand eight hundred and twenty-one.	

TABLE LIII.

Words of the same sound, but different in spelling and signification.

AIL, to be troubled
Ale, malt liquor
Air, an element
Are, plural of is or am
Heir, to an estate
All, the whole
Awl, an instrument
Al tar, for sacrifice
Al ter, to change
Ant, a pismire
Aunt, uncle's wife
As cent, steepness
As sent, an agreement
Au ger, an instrument
Au gur, one who foretells
Bail, surety
Bale, a pack of goods
Ball, a round substance
Bawl, to cry aloud
Bare, naked
Bear, to suffer
Bear, a beast
Base, vile
Bass, in music
Beer, a liquor
Bier, to carry the dead
Ber ry, a small fruit
Bu ry, to inter the dead
Beat, to strike
Beet, a root
Blew, did blow
Blue, colour
Boar, a male swine
Bore, to make a hole
Bow, to bend
Bough, a branch

Bow, to shoot with
Beau, a gay fellow
Bred, brought up
Bread, food
Bur row, for rabbits
Bor ough, a town corpo-
    rate
By, a particle
Buy, to purchase
Cain, a man's name
Cane, a shrub or staff
Call, to cry out
Caul, of a wig or bowels
Can non, a large gun
Can on, a rule
Can vass, to examine
Can vas, coarse cloth
Ceil ing, of a room
Seal ing, setting of a seal
Cell, a hut
Sell, to dispose of
Cen tu ry, a hundred
    years
Cen tau ry, an herb
Chol er, wrath
Col lar, for the neck
Cord, a small rope
Chord, in music
Ci on, a young shoot
Si on, a mountain
Cite, to summon
Sight, seeing
Site, situation
Chron i cal, of a long con-
    tinuance
Chron i cle, a history

Course, order or direction
Coarse, not fine
Com ple ment, a full num-
ber
Com pli ment, expression of
civility
Cous in, a relation
Coz en, to cheat
Coun cil, an assembly
Coun sel, advice
Cur rant, a berry
Cur rent, passing, or a
stream
Deer, a wild animal
Dear, of great price
Dew, from heaven
Due, owed
Die, to expire
Dye, to color
Doe, a female deer
Dough, bread unbaked
Dun, brown color
Done performed
Fane, a weathercock
Fain, gladly
Feign, to dissemble
Faint, weary
Feint, a false march
Fair, comely
Fare, food, customary du-
ty, &c.
Fel lon, a whitlow
Fel on, a criminal
Flee, an insect
Flee, to run away
Flour, of wheat
Flow er, of the field
Fourth, in number
Forth, abroad
Foul, nasty
Fowl, a bird

Gilt, with gold
Guilt, crime
Grate, for coals
Great, large
Groan, to sigh
Grown, increased
Hail, to salute, or frozen
drops of rain
Hale, sound, healthy
Hart, a beast
Heart, the seat of life
Hare, an animal
Hair, of the head
Here, in this place
Hear, to hearken
Hew, to cut
Hue, color
Him, that man
Hymn, a sacred song
Hire, wages
High er, more high
Heel, of the foot
Heal, to cure
I, myself
Eye, organ of sight
Isle, an island
Ile, of a church
In, within
Inn, a tavern
In dite, to compose
In dict, to prosecute
Kill, to slay
Kiln, of brick
Knave, a dishonest man
Nave, of a wheel
Knight, by honor
Night, the evening
Know, to be acquainted
No, not so
Knew, did know
New, not old

Knot, made by tying
Not, denying
Lade, to dip water
Laid, placed
Lain, did lie
Lane, a narrow passage
Leek, a root
Leak, to run out
Les son, a reading
Les sen, to diminish
Li ar, a teller of lies
Lyre, a harp
Led, did lead
Lead, heavy metal
Lie, a falsehood, also to rest
  on a bed
Lye, water drained through
  ashes
Lo, behold
Low, humble
Made, finished
Maid, an unmarried woman
Main, the chief
Mane, of a horse
Male, the he kind
Mail, armor, or a packet
Man ner, mode or custom
Man or, a lordship
Meet, to come together
Meat, flesh
Mete, measure
Mite, an insect
Might, strength
Met al, gold, silver, &c.
Met tle, briskness
Naught, bad
Nought, none
Nay, no
Neigh, as a horse
Oar, to row with
Ore, metal not separated

Oh, alas
Owe, to be indebted
One, in number
Won, past time of *win*
Our, belonging
Hour, sixty minutes
Pale, wanting color
Pail, a vessel
Pain, torment
Pane, a square of glass
Peel, the outside
Peal, upon the bells
Pear, a fruit
Pare, to cut off
Plain, even, or level
Plane, to make smooth
Plate, a flat piece of metal
Plait, a fold in a garment
Pray, to implore
Prey, a booty
Prin ci pal, chief
Prin ci ple, first rule
Proph et, a foreteller
Prof it, advantage
Peace, tranquillity
Piece, a part
Rain, falling water
Rein, of a bridle
Reign, to rule
Reed, a shrub
Read, to peruse
Rest, ease
Wrest, to force
Rice, a sort of corn
Rise, origin
Rye, a sort of grain
Wry, crooked
Ring, to sound
Wring, to twist
Rite, ceremony
Right, just

Write, to form letters with
    a pen
Wright, a workman
  Rode, did ride
  Road, the highway
Roe, a deer
Row, a rank
  Ruff, a neckcloth
  Rough, not smooth
Sail, of a ship
Sale, a selling
  Seen, beheld
  Scene, of a stage
See, to behold
Sea, the ocean
  Sent, ordered away
  Scent, smell
Senior, elder
Seignior, a lord
  Shore, side of a river
  Shoar, a prop
Sink, to go down
Cinque, five
  So, thus
  Sow, to scatter
Sum, the whole
Scene, a part
  Sun, the fountain of light
  Son, a male child
Sore, an ulcer
Soar, to mount up
  Stare, to look earnestly
  Stair, a step
Steel, hard metal
Steal, to take without lib-
    erty
  Succor, help
  Sucker, a young twig
Sleight, dexterity
Slight, to despise

Sole, of the foot
Soul, the spirit
Tax, a rate
Tacks, small nails
Tale, a story
Tail, the end
Tare, weight allowed
Tear, to rend
  Team, of cattle or horses
  Teem, to go with young
Their, belonging to them
There, in that place
The, a particle
Thee, yourself
Too, likewise
Two, twice one
  Tow, to drag after
  Toe, of the foot
Vale, a valley
Veil, a covering
  Vein, for the blood
  Vane, to shew the course
    of the wind
Vice, sin
Vise, a screw
  Wait, to tarry
  Weight, heaviness
Wear, to put on
Ware, merchandise
Were, past time plural of *am*
  Waste, to spend
  Waist, the middle
Way, road
Weigh, to poise
  Week, seven days
  Weak, not strong
Wood, trees
Would, was willing
  You, plural of *thee*
  Yew, a tree

TABLE LIV.

Of Abbreviations.

A. A. S. Fellow of the American Academy
C. A. S. Fellow of the Connecticut Academy
A. B. Bachelor of Arts
A. D. In the year of our Lord
A. M. Master of Arts, before noon, or in the year of the world
Bart. Baronet
B. D Bachelor of Divinity
C. or Cent. a hundred
Capt. Captain
Col. Colonel
Cant. Canticles
Chap. Chapter
Chron. Chronicles
Co Company
Com. Commissioner
Cr. Credit
Cwt. Hundred weight
D. D. Doctor of Divinity
Dr. Doctor or Debtor
Dec. December
Dep Deputy
Deut. Deuteronomy
Do. or ditto, the same
E. G. for example
Eccl. Ecclesiastes
Ep. Epistle
Eng. English
Eph. Ephesians
Esa. Esaias
Ex. Example, or Exodus
Feb. February
Fr. France, or Francis

F. R. S. Fellow of the Royal Society
Gal. Galatians
Gen. Genesis
Gent. Gentleman
Geo. George
G. R. George the King
Heb. Hebrews
Hon. Honorable
Hund. Hundred
Ibidem, ibid. in the same place
Isa. Isaiah
i. e. that is
Id. the same
Jan. January
Ja. James
Jac. Jacob
Josh. Joshua
K. King
Km. Kingdom
Kt. Knight
L. Lord or Lady
Lev. Leviticus
Lieut. Lieutenant
L. L. D. Doctor of Laws
L. S. the place of the Seal
Lond. London
M. Marquis
M. B. Bachelor of Physic
M. D. Doctor of Physic
Mr. Master
Messrs. Gentlemen, Sirs
Mrs. Mistress
M. S. Manuscript
M. S. S. Manuscripts
Mat. Matthew

Math. Mathematics

N. B. take particular notice

Nov. November

No. Number

N. S. New Stile

Obj. Objection

Oct. October

O. S. Old Stile

Parl. Parliament

Per cent. by the hundred

Pet. Peter

Phil. Philip

Philom. a lover of learning

P. M. Afternoon

P. S. Postscript

Ps. Psalm

Q. Question, Queen

q d. as if he should say

q. l. as much as you please

Regr. Register

Rev. Revelation, Reverend

Rt. Hon. Right Honorable

S. South and Shilling

St. Saint

Sept. September

Serj. Sergeant

S. T. P. Professor of Divinity

S. T. D. Doctor of Divinity

ss. to wit, namely

Theo. Theophilus

Tho. Thomas

Thess. Thessalonians

V. or vide, see

Viz. to wit. namely

Wm. William

Wp. Worship

&. and

&c. and so forth

U. S. A. United States of America

EXPLANATION

Of the Pauses *and other* Characters *used in* Writing.

A comma, (,) is a pause of one syllable—A semicolon, (;) two—A colon (:) four—A period (.) six—An interrogation point (?) shows when a question is asked ; as, *What do you see?* An exclamation point (!) is a mark of wonder or surprise ; as, *O the folly of sinners!*—The pause of these two points is the same as a colon or a period, and the sentence should usually be closed with a raised tone of voice.

( ) A parenthesis includes a part of a sentence, which is not necessary to make sense, and should be read quicker, and in a weaker tone of voice.

[ ] Brackets or Hooks, include words that serve to explain a foregoing word or sentence.

- A Hyphen joins words or syllables ; as, *sea-water.*

' An Apostrophe shows when a letter is omitted as *us'd* for used.

⌃ A caret shows when a word or number of words are omitted through mistake ; as, *this is ^my^ book.*

" A quotation or double comma, includes a passage that is taken from some other author in his own words.

☞ The index points to some remarkable passage.

¶ The paragraph begins a new subject.

§ The section is used to divide chapters.

*†‡‖ An asterisk, and other references, point to a note in the margin or bottom of a page.

OF CAPITAL LETTERS.

Sentences should begin with a capital letter—also every line in poetry. Proper names, which are the names of persons, places, rivers, mountains, lakes, &c. should begin with a capital. Also the name of the Supreme Being.

ADDITIONAL LESSONS.
DOMESTIC ECONOMY,

Or, the History of THRIFTY *and* UNTHRIFTY.

THERE is a great difference among men, in their ability to gain property ; but a still greater difference in their power of using it to advantage. Two men may acquire the same amount of money, in a given time ; yet one will prove to be a poor man, while the other becomes rich. A chief and essential difference in the management of property, is, that one man spends only the *interest* of his money, while another spends the *principal.*

I know a farmer by the name of THRIFTY, who manages his affairs in this manner : He rises early in the morning, looks to the condition of his house, barn, home-lot and stock—sees that his cattle, horses and hogs are fed, examines the tools to see whether they are all in good order for the workmen—takes care that breakfast is ready in due season, and begins work in the cool of the day—When in the field, he keeps steadily at work, though not so violently as to fatigue and exhaust the body—nor does he stop to tell or hear long stories—When the labor of the day is past, he takes refreshment, and goes to rest at an early hour.—In this manner he earns and gains money.

When *Thrifty* has acquired a little property, he does not spend it or let it slip from him, without use or benefit. He pays his taxes and debts when due or called for, so that he has no officers fees to pay, nor expenses of courts. He does not frequent the tavern and drink up all his earnings in liquor that does him no good. He puts his money to use, that is, he buys more land, or stock, or lends his money at interest—in short, he makes his money produce some profit or income. These savings and profits, though small by themselves, amount in a year to a considerable sum, and in a few years, they swell to an estate—Thrifty becomes a wealthy farmer, with several hundred acres of land, and a hundred head of cattle.

Very different is the management of UNTHRIFTY: He lies in bed till a late hour in the morning—then rises, and goes to the bottle for a dram, or to the tavern for a glass of bitters—Thus he spends six cents before breakfast, for a dram that makes him dull and heavy all day. He gets his breakfast late, when he ought to be at work—When he supposes he is ready to begin the work of the day, he finds he has not the necessary tools, or some of them are out of order,—the plow-share is to be sent half a mile to a blacksmith to be mended; a tooth or two in a rake, or the handle of a hoe is broke; or a sythe or an ax is to be ground.—Now, he is in a great hurry, he bustles about to make preparation for work—and what is done in a hurry is ill done—he loses a part of the day in getting ready—and perhaps the time of his workmen. At ten or eleven o'clock, he is ready to go to work—then comes a boy and tells him, the sheep have escaped from the pasture—or the cows have got among his corn—or the hogs into the garden: He frets and storms, and runs to drive them out—a half hour or more time is lost in driving the cattle from mischief, and repairing a poor broken fence; a fence that answers no purpose but to lull him into security, and teach his horses and cattle to be unruly. After all this bustle, the fatigue of which is worse than common labor, *Unthrifty* is ready to begin a day's work at twelve o'clock.—Thus half his time is lost in supplying defects, which proceed from want of foresight and good management. His small crops are damaged or destroyed by unruly cattle.—His barn is open and leaky, and what little he gathers. is injured by the rain and snow.—His house is in a like condition—the shingles and clapboards fall off and let in the water, which causes the timber, floors and furniture to decay—and exposed to inclemencies of weather, his wife and children fall sick—their time is lost, and the mischief closes with a ruinous train of expenses for medicines and physicians.—After dragging out some years of disappointment, misery and poverty, the lawyer and the sheriff sweep away the scanty remains of his estate. This is the history of UNTHRIFTY—his principal is spent—he has no interest.

Not unlike this, is the history of the Grog-drinker. This man wonders why he does not thrive in the world; he cannot see the reason why his neighbor *Temperance* should be more prosperous than himself—but in truth, he makes no calculations. Ten cents a day for grog, is a small sum, he thinks, which can hurt no man! But let us make an estimate—arithmetic is very useful for a man who ventures to spend small sums every day. Ten cents a day amount in a year to thirty-six dollars and a half—a sum sufficient to buy a good farm horse! This surely is no small sum for a farmer or mechanic—But in ten years, this sum amounts to three hundred and sixty five dollars, besides interest in the mean time! What an amount is this for drams and bitters in ten years! it is money enough to build a small house! But look at the amount in thirty years!—One thousand and ninety five dollars! What a vast sum to run down one man's throat in liquor—a sum that will buy a farm sufficient to maintain a small family Suppose a family to consume a quart of spirits in a day, at twenty-five cents a quart. The amount of this in a year, is ninety-one dollars and a quarter—in ten years, nine hundred and twelve dollars and a half—and in thirty years, two thousand seven hundred and thirty seven dollars and a half! A great estate may thus be consumed in a single quart of rum! What mischief is done by the love of spirituous liquors!

But, says the laboring man, " I cannot work without spirits—I must have something to give me strength." Then drink something that will give durable nourishment—Of all the substances taken into the stomach, spirituous liquors contain the least nutriment, and add the least to bodily vigor. Malt liquors, molasses and water, milk and water, contain nutriment, and even cider is not wholly destitute of it—but distilled spirituous liquors contain little or none.

But, says the laborer or the traveller, " spirituous liquors warm the stomach, and are very useful in cold weather"—No, this is not correct. Spirits enliven the feelings for half an hour---but leave the body more dull, languid and cold than it was before. A man will freeze the sooner for drinking spirits of any kind. If a man wishes to guard against cold, let him eat a biscuit, a bit of bread, or a meal of victuals. Four ounces of bread will give a more durable warmth to the body, than a gallon of spirits—food is the natural stimulant or exciting power of the human body—it gives warmth and strength, and does not leave the body, as spirit does, more feeble and languid. —The practice of drinking spirits gives a man red eyes, a bloated face, and an empty purse—It injures the liver, produces dropsy, occasions a trembling of the joints and limbs, and closes life with a slow decay or palsy.—This is a short history of the drinker of distilled spirits—If a few drinking men are found to be exceptions to this account, still the remarks are true, as they apply to most cases. Spirituous liquors shorten more lives than famine, pestilence and the sword!

LESSONS on FAMILIAR SUBJECTS.

ALL mankind live on the fruits of the earth—the first and most necessary employment therefore is the tillage of the ground, called agriculture, husbandry, or farming. The farmer clears his land of trees, roots and stones—he surrounds it with a fence of poles, posts and rails, stone-wall, hedge or ditch. He plows and harrows, or drags the soil, to break the clods or turf, and make it mellow and pliable ; he manures it also, if necessary, with stable dung, ashes, marl, plaster, lime, sea-shells, or decayed vegetable substances. He plants maize in rows, or sows wheat, barley, rye, oats, buckwheat, flax or hemp. He hoes the maize, two or three times, kills the weeds, and draws the earth round the hills to support and nourish the plants—When the grain is ripe, he reaps or cradles his grain, and pulls the flax. The ears of maize are picked by hand, or the stalks cut with a sickle or knife, and the husks are stripped off, in the evening. With what joy does the farmer gather his crops, of the former and latter harvest!—He toils indeed, but he reaps the fruit of his labor in peace—he fills his granary in summer, and in autumn presents a thank-offering to God for his bounty.

See the mower, how he swings his sythe!—The grass falls prostrate before him—the glory of the field is laid low—the land is stripped of its verdant covering. See the stripling follow his father or brother, and with a pitchfork, spread the thick swath, and shake the grass about the meadow! How fragrant the smell of new made hay—how delightful the task to tend it!

Enter the forest of the wilderness—See here and there a rustic dwelling made of logs—a little spot cleared and cultivated—a thatched hovel to shelter a cow and her food—the forest resounding with the ax-man's blows, as he levels the sturdy beach, maple, or hemlock; while the crackling fire aids his hands, by consuming the massy piles of wood which he cannot remove—Hear the howling wolf, or watch the nimble deer, as he bounds along among the trees—The faithful cow, in search of shrubs and twigs, strays from the cottage, and the owner seeks her at evening, in the gloomy forest; led by the tinkling of the bell, he finds and drives her home. A bowl of bread and milk, furnishes him with his frugal repast, he retires weary to rest—and the sleep of the laboring man is sweet.

See the dairy-woman, while she fills her pails with new milk—the gentle cows quietly chewing their cuds by her side. Enter the milk-room, see the pans, pails and tubs, how clean and sweet, all in order, and fit for use! The milk strained and put in a cool place—the cream skimmed off for butter, or the milk set for cheese.

—Here is a churn as white as ivory —there a cheese-press forcing the whey from the curd! See the shelves filled with cheeses—What a noble sight! and butter as yellow as the purest gold!

George, let us look into the work-shops among the mechanics. Here is a carpenter, he squares a post or a beam; he scores or notches it first, and then hews it with his broad-ax. He bores holes with an auger, and with the help of a chisel, forms a mortise for a tenon. He measures with a square or rule, and marks his work with a compass. Each timber is fitted to its place. The sills support the posts, and these support the beams. Braces secure the frame of a building from swaying or leaning—Girders and joists support the floors; studs, with the posts, support the walls, and rafters uphold the roof.

Now comes the joiner with his chest of tools. He planes the boards, joints the shingles and covers the building—With his saw he cuts boards, with his gimblet or wimble, he makes holes for nails, pins or spikes,—with his chisel and gouge, he makes mortises.

Then comes the mason with his trowel—the laths are nailed to the studs and joists to support the plaster, first a rough coat of coarse mortar of lime and sand is laid on, and this is covered with a beautiful white plaster. And last of all comes the painter with his brush and oil-pots —he mixes the oil and white lead, and gives to the apartments the color which the owner or his lady sees fit to direct.

A MORAL CATECHISM.

Question. *WHAT is moral virtue?*

Answer. It is an honest upright conduct in all our dealings with men.

Q. *What rules have we to direct us in our moral conduct?*

A. GOD's word, contained in the bible, has furnished all necessary rules to direct our conduct.

Q. *In what part of the bible are these rules to be found?*

A. In almost every part; but the most important duties between men are summed up in the beginning of Matthew, in CHRIST's Sermon on the Mount.

Of HUMILITY.

Q. *What is humility?*

A. A lowly temper of mind.

Q. *What are the advantages of humility?*

A. The advantages of humility in this life are very numerous and great. The humble man has few or no enemies. Every one loves him and is ready to do him good. If he is rich and prosperous, people do not envy him ; if he is poor and unfortunate, every one pities him, and is disposed to alleviate his distresses.

Q. *What is pride?*

A. A lofty high-minded disposition.

Q. *Is pride commendable?*

A. By no means. A modest, self-approving opinion of our own good deeds is very right—it is natural—it is agreeable, and a spur to good actions. But we should not suffer our hearts to be blown up with pride, whatever great and good deeds we have done ; for pride brings upon us the ill-will of mankind, and displeasure of our Maker.

Q. *What effect has humility upon our own minds?*

A. Humility is attended with peace of mind and self-satisfaction. The humble man is not disturbed with cross accidents, and is never fretful and uneasy ; nor does he repine when others grow rich. He is contented, because his mind is at ease.

Q. *What is the effect of pride on a man's happiness?*

A. Pride exposes a man to numberless disappointments and mortifications. The proud man expects more attention and respect will be paid to him, than he deserves, or than others are willing to pay him. He is neglected, laughed at and despised, and this treatment frets him, so that his own mind becomes a seat of torment. A proud man cannot be a happy man.

Q. *What has Christ said, respecting the virtue of humility?*

A. He has said, "blessed are the poor in spirit, for theirs is the kingdom of heaven." Poorness of spirit is humility ; and this humble temper prepares a man for heaven, where all is peace and love

OF MERCY.

Q. What is mercy?

A. It is tenderness of heart.

Q. What are the advantages of this virtue?

A. The exercise of it tends to diffuse happiness and lessen the evils of life. Rulers of a merciful temper will make their *good* subjects happy ; and will not torment the *bad*, with needless severity. Parents and masters will not abuse their children and servants with harsh treatment. More love, more confidence, more happiness, will subsist among men, and of course society will be happier.

Q. Should not beasts as well as men be treated with mercy?

A. They ought indeed. It is wrong to give needless pain even to a beast. Cruelty to the brutes shows a man has a hard heart, and if a man is unfeeling to a beast, he will not have much feeling for men. If a man treats his beast with cruelty, beware of trusting yourself in his power. He will probably make a severe master and a cruel husband.

Q. How does cruelty shew its effects?

A. A cruel disposition is usually exercised upon those who are under its power. Cruel rulers make severe laws which injure the persons and properties of their subjects. Cruel officers execute laws in a severe manner, when it is not necessary for public good. A cruel husband abuses his wife and children. A cruel master acts the tyrant over his apprentices and servants. The effects of cruelty are, hatred, quarrels, tumults, and wretchedness.

Q. What does Christ say of the merciful man?

A. He says he is " blessed, for he shall obtain mercy." He who shows mercy and tenderness to others, will be treated with tenderness and compassion himself.

OF PEACE-MAKERS.

Q. Who are peace-makers?

A. All who endeavor to prevent quarrels and disputes among men , or to reconcile those who are separated by strife.

Q. Is it unlawful to contend with others on any occasion?

A. It is impossible to avoid some differences with

men ; disputes should be always conducted with temper and moderation. The man who keeps his temper will not be rash, and do or say things which he will afterwards repent of. And though men should sometimes differ, still they should be friends. They should be ready to do kind offices to each other.

Q. *What is the reward of the peace-maker?*

A. He shall be " blessed, and called the child of God." The mild, peaceable, friendly man, resembles God. What an amiable character is this! To be like our heavenly Father, that lovely, perfect and glorious being, who is the source of all good, is to be the best and happiest of men.

Of PURITY of HEART.

Q. *What is a pure heart?*

A. A heart free from all bad desires, and inclined to conform to the divine will in all things.

Q. *Should a man's intentions as well as his actions be good?*

A. Most certainly. Actions cannot be called *good*, unless they proceed from good motives. We should wish to see, and to make all men better and happier—we should rejoice at their prosperity. This is benevolence.

Q. *What reward is promised to the pure in heart?*

A. Christ has declared " they shall see God." A pure heart is like God, and those who possess it shall dwell in his presence and enjoy his favor for ever.

Of ANGER.

Q. *Is it right ever to be angry?*

A. It is right in certain cases that we should be angry ; as when gross affronts are offered to us, and injuries done us by design. A suitable spirit of resentment, in such cases, will obtain justice for us, and protect us from further insults.

Q. *By what rule should anger be governed?*

A. We should never be angry without a cause ; that is, we should be certain a person *means* to affront, injure or insult us, before we suffer ourselves to be angry. It is wrong, it is mean, it is a mark of a little mind, to take fire at every little trifling dispute. And when we have real cause to be angry we should observe moderation.   We should never be in a passion.   A passionate man is like a madman, and is always inexcusable.   We should be cool even in anger ; and be angry no longer than to obtain justice.   In short, we should " be angry and sin not."

Of REVENGE.

Q. *What is revenge?*

A. It is to injure a man because he has injured us.

Q. *Is this justifiable?*

A. Never, in any possible case.   Revenge is perhaps the meanest, as well as the wickedest vice in society.

Q. *What shall a man do to obtain justice when he is injured?*

A. In general, laws have made provision for doing justice to every man ; and it is right and honorable, when a man is injured, that he should seek a recompense. But a recompense is all he can demand, and of that he should not be his own judge, but should submit the matter to judges appointed by authority.

Q. *But suppose a man insults us in such a manner that the law cannot give us redress?*

A. Then forgive him.   " If a man strikes you on one cheek, turn the other to him," and let him repeat the abuse, rather than strike him.

Q. *But if we are in danger from the blows of another, may we not defend ourselves?*

A. Most certainly.   We have always a right to defend our persons, property, and families.   But we have no right to fight and abuse people merely for revenge.   It is nobler to forgive.   " Love your enemies—bless them that curse you—do good to them that hate you—pray for them that use you ill,"—these are the commands of the blessed Savior of men.   The man who does this is great and good ; he is as much above the little, mean, revengeful man, as virtue is above vice, or as heaven is higher than hell.

Of JUSTICE.

Q. *What is justice?*

A. It is giving to every man his due.

Q. *Is it always easy to know what is just?*

A. It is generally easy ; and where there is any diffi

culty in determining, let a man consult the golden rule —" To do to others, what he could reasonably wish they should do to him, in the same circumstances."

Q. *What are the ill effects of injustice?*

A. If a man does injustice, or rather, if he refuses to do justice, he must be compelled. Then follows a law-suit, with a series of expenses, and what is worse, ill-blood and enmity between the parties. Somebody is always the worse for law-suits, and of course society is less happy.

Of GENEROSITY.

Q. *What is generosity?*

A. It is some act of kindness performed for another which strict justice does not demand.

Q. *Is this a virtue?*

A. It is indeed a noble virtue. To do justice, is well; but to do more than justice, is still better, and may proceed from nobler motives.

Q. *What has Christ said respecting generosity?*

A. He has commanded us to be generous in this passage, " Whosoever shall compel (or urge) you to go a *mile*, go with him *two*."

Q. *Are we to perform this literally?*

A. The meaning of this command will not always require this.—But in general we are to do more for others than they ask, provided we can do it without essentially injuring ourselves. We ought cheerfully to suffer many inconveniences to oblige others, though we are not required to do ourselves any essential injury.

Q. *Of what advantage is generosity to the man who exercises it?*

A. It lays others under obligations to the generous man; and the probability is, that he will be repaid three fold. Every man on earth wants favors at some time or other in his life; and if we will not help others, others will not help us. It is for a man's interest to be generous.

Q. *Ought we to do kind actions because it is for our interest?*

A. This may be a motive at all times; but if it is the principal motive, it is less honorable. We ought to do good, as we have opportunity, at all times and to all men, whether we expect a reward or not; for if we do good, somebody is the happier for it. This alone is reason enough, why we should do all the good in our power.

Of GRATITUDE.

Q. *What is gratitude?*

A. A thankfulness of heart for favors received.

Q. *Is it a duty to be thankful for favors?*

A. It is a duty and a virtue. A man who does not feel grateful for kind acts done for him by others, does not deserve favors of any kind. He ought to be shut out from the society of the good. He is worse than a savage, for a savage never forgets an act of kindness.

Q. *What is the effect of true kindness?*

A. It softens the heart towards the generous man; and every thing which subdues the pride and other unsocial passions of the heart, fits a man to be a better citizen, a better neighbor, a better husband, and a better friend. A man who is sensible of favors, and ready to acknowledge them, is more inclined to perform kind offices, not only towards his benefactor, but towards all others.

Of TRUTH.

Q. *What is truth?*

A. It is speaking and acting agreeable to fact.

Q. *Is it a duty to speak truth at all times?*

A. If we speak at all, we should tell the truth. It is not always necessary to tell what we know. There are many things which concern ourselves and others which we had better not publish to the world.

Q. *What rules are there respecting the publishing of truth?*

A. 1. When we are called upon to testify in courts, we should speak the whole truth, and that without disguise. To leave out small circumstances, or to give a coloring to others, with a view to favor one side more than the other, is to the highest degree criminal.

2. When we know something of our neighbor which

is against his character, we may not publish it, unless to prevent his doing an injury to another person.

3. When we sell any thing to another, we ought not to represent the article to be better than it really is. If there are faults in it which may easily be seen, the law of man does not require us to inform the buyer of these faults, because he may see them himself. But it is not honorable nor generous, nor strictly honest, to conceal even apparent faults. But when faults are out of sight, the seller ought to tell the buyer of them. If he does not, he is a cheat and a downright knave.

Q. *What are the ill effects of lying and deceiving?*

A. The man who lies, deceives or cheats, loses his reputation. No person will believe him, even when he speaks the truth; he is shunned as a pest to society.

Falsehood and cheating destroy all confidence between man and man; they raise jealousies and suspicions among men; they thus weaken the bands of society and destroy happiness. Besides, cheating often strips people of their property, and makes them poor and wretched.

OF CHARITY AND GIVING ALMS.

Q. *What is charity?*

A. It signifies giving to the poor, or it is a favorable opinion of men and their actions.

Q. *When and how far is it our duty to give to the poor?*

A. When others really want what we can spare without material injury to ourselves, it is our duty to give them something to relieve their wants.

Q. *When persons are reduced to want by their own laziness and vices, by drunkenness, gambling, and the like, is it a duty to relieve them?*

A. In general, it is not. The man who gives money and provisions to a lazy, vicious man, becomes a partaker of his guilt. Perhaps it may be right, to give such a man a meal of victuals to keep him from starving, and it is certainly right to feed his wife and family, and make them comfortable.

Q. *Who are the proper objects of charity?*

A. Persons who are reduced to want by sickness, unavoidable losses by fire, storms at sea or land, drouth or accidents of other kinds. To such persons we are commanded to give ; and it is our own interest to be charitable ; for we are all liable to misfortunes, and may want charity ourselves.

Q. *In what manner should we bestow favors?*

A. We should do it with gentleness and affection ; putting on no airs of pride and arrogance. We should also take no pains to publish our charities, but rather to conceal them ; for if we boast of our generosity, we discover that we give from mean, selfish motives. Christ commands us, in giving alms, not to let our left hand know what our right hand doeth.

Q. *How can charity be exercised in our opinions of others?*

A. By thinking favorably of them and their actions. Every man has his faults ; but charity will not put a harsh construction on another's conduct. It will not charge his conduct to bad views and motives, unless this appears very clear indeed.

Of AVARICE.

Q. *What is avarice?*

A. An excessive desire of possessing wealth.

Q. *Is this commendable?*

A. It is not ; but one of the meanest of vices.

Q. *Can an avaricious man be an honest man?*

A. It is hardly possible ; for the lust of gain is almost always accompanied with a disposition to take mean and undue advantages of others.

Q. *What effect has avarice upon the heart?*

A. It contracts the heart—narrows the sphere of benevolence—blunts all the fine feelings of sensibility, and sours the mind towards society. An avaricious man, a miser, a niggard, is wrapped up in selfishness, like some worms, which crawl about and eat for some time to fill *themselves*, then wind themselves up in separate coverings and die.

Q. *What injury is done by avarice to society?*

A. Avarice gathers together more property than the owner wants, and keeps it hoarded up, where it does no good. The poor are thus deprived of some business, some means of support; the property gains nothing to the community; and somebody is less happy by means of this hoarding of wealth.

Q. *In what proportion does avarice do hurt?*

A. In an exact proportion to its power of doing good. The miser's *heart* grows *less*, in proportion as his *estate* grows *larger*. The more money he has, the more he has people in his power, and the more he grinds the face of the poor. The larger the tree and the more spreading the branches, the more small plants are shaded and robbed of their nourishment.

Of FRUGALITY and ECONOMY.

Q. *What is the distinction between frugality and avarice?*

A. Frugality is a prudent saving of property from needless waste. Avarice gathers more and spends less than is necessary.

Q. *What is economy?*

A. It is frugality in expenses—it is a prudent management of one's estate. It disposes of property for useful purposes without waste.

Q. *How far does true economy extend?*

A. To the saving of every thing which it is not necessary to spend for comfort and convenience; and the keeping one's expenses within his income or earnings.

Q. *What is wastefulness?*

A. It is the spending of money for what is not wanted. If a man drinks a dram which is not necessary for him, or buys a cane which he does not want, he wastes his money. He injures *himself*, as much as if he had thrown away his money.

Q. *Is not waste often occasioned by mere negligence?*

A. Very often. The man who does not keep his house and barn well covered; who does not keep good fences about his fields; who suffers his farming utensils to lie out in the rain or on the ground; or his cattle to waste manure in the high way, is as much a spendthrift as the tavern haunter, the tippler, and the gamester.

Q. Do not careless, slovenly people, work harder than the neat and orderly?

A. Much harder. It is more labor to destroy a growth of sturdy weeds, than to pull them up when they first spring from the ground. So the disorders and abuses which grow out of a sloven's carelessness, in time, become almost incurable. Hence such people work like slaves, and to little effect.

Of INDUSTRY.

Q. What is industry?

It is a diligent attention to business in our several occupations.

Q. Is labor a curse or a blessing?

A. Hard labor or drudgery is often a curse, by making life toilsome and painful. But constant moderate labor is the greatest of blessings.

Q. Why then do people complain of it?

A. Because they do not know the evils of *not* laboring. Labor keeps the body in health, and makes men relish all their enjoyments. "The sleep of the laboring man is sweet," so is his food. He walks cheerful and whistling about his field or his shop, and scarcely knows pain.

The rich and indolent first lose their health for want of action—They turn pale, their bodies are enfeebled, they lose their appetite for food and sleep, they yawn out a tasteless life of dullness, without pleasure, and often useless to the world.

Q. What are the other good effects of industry?

A. One effect is to procure an estate. Our Creator, has kindly united our duty, our interest, and happiness; for the same labor which makes us healthy and cheerful, gives wealth.

Another good effect of industry is, to keep men from vice. Not all the moral discourses ever delivered to mankind, have so much effect in checking the bad passions of men, in keeping order and peace, and maintaining moral virtue in society, as *industry.* *Business* is a source of health, of prosperity, of virtue, and obedience to law. To make good subjects and good citizens, the first requisite is to educate every young person, in some kind of business. The possession of millions should not excuse a young man from application to business; and that parent or guardian who suffers his child or his ward to be bred in idleness, becomes accessary to the vices and disorders of society—He is guilty of " not providing for his household, and is worse than an infidel."

Of CHEERFULNESS.

Q. Is cheerfulness a virtue?

A. It doubtless is, and a moral duty to practice it.

Q. Can we be cheerful when we please?

A. In general it depends much on ourselves. We can often mold our tempers into a cheerful frame.—We can frequent company and other objects calculated to inspire us with cheerfulness. To indulge an habitual gloominess of mind is weakness and sin.

Q. What are the effects of cheerfulness on ourselves?

A. Cheerfulness is a great preservative of health, over which it is our duty to watch with care. We have no right to sacrifice our health by the indulgence of a gloomy state of mind. Besides, a cheerful man will do more business, and do it better, than a melancholy one.

Q. What are the effects of cheerfulness on others?

A. Cheerfulness is readily communicated to others, by which means their happiness is increased. We are all influenced by sympathy, and naturally partake of the joys and sorrows of others.

Q. What effect has melancholy on the heart?

A. It hardens and benumbs it—It chills the warm affections of love and friendship, and prevents the exercise of the social passions. A melancholy person's life is all night and winter. It is as unnatural as perpetual darkness and frost.

Q. What shall one do when overwhelmed with grief?

A. The best method of expelling grief from the mind,

or of quieting its pains, is to change the objects that are about us ; to ride from place to place, and frequent cheerful company. It is our duty so to do, especially when grief sits heavy on the heart.

Q. Is it not right to grieve for the loss of our friends?

A. It is certainly right ; but we should endeavor to moderate our grief, and not suffer it to impair our health, or to grow into a settled melancholy. The use of grief is to soften the heart and make us better. But when our friends are dead, we can render them no further service. Our duty to them ends, when we commit them to the grave ; f at our duty to ourselves, our families and sur- viving friends, requires that we perform to them the cus- tomary offices of life. We should therefore remember our departed friends only to imitate their virtues ; and not to pine away with useless sorrow.

Q. Has not religion a tendency to fill the mind with gloom?

A. True religion never has this effect. Superstition and false notions of God, often make men gloomy ; but true rational piety and religion have the contrary effect. They fill the mind with joy and cheerfulness ; and the countenance of a truly pious man should always wear a serene smile.

Q. What has Christ said concerning gloomy Christians?

A. He has pronounced them hypocrites ; and com- manded his followers not to copy their sad countenances and disfigured faces ; but even in their acts of humilia- tion to " anoint their heads and wash their feet." Christ intended by this, that religion does not consist in, nor re- quire a monkish sadness and gravity ; on the other hand, he intimates that such *appearances* of sanctity are gener- ally the marks of hypocrisy. He expressly enjoins upon his foll wers marks of cheerfulness. Indeed, the only true ground of perpetual cheerfulness, is, a conscious- ness of ever having done well, and an assurance of divine favor

FINIS.